SOVEREIGN *unto* HE

FLOWER *of* LIFE PRESS

Praise

"All I can say is wow! *Rima Bonario's chapter on Sexual Sovereignty in* Sovereign Unto Herself *has opened my heart to a radically different understanding of what was happening for me. The idea of shifting our energetic polarity instead of finding someone to blame is life-changing. As women, we've come to view our bodies as just a vehicle for getting stuff done. What a gift to know it's not only possible, but completely natural to have a beautiful, fulfilling sex life for as long you stay committed to the practice of honoring your own feminine energy."*

—Cyndi A. Swall, Executive Coach, Speaker, Bliss Mentor, and Author of *Bliss in the Wild*

"In her chapter, 'Artist ascension,' Alexis Cohen reveals the enchanted path to our deepest visions. We are taken on a journey of reclamation, inspiration, and deep listening... every visionary woman artist will find her powerful voice again here. It's as if the words themselves ignite a fire deep within your Heart, as you recall why you came to Earth in the first place!"

—Christina Marie Miglino, Energy Intuitive, Shamanic Guide, Golden Goddess, Channel of The3, 'Collaborations With Spirit' private Facebook Community

"MaryAiñe Curtis' powerful testimony about the re-emergence of her own inner Sovereign Queen will light the flame of self-recognition, self-compassion and self-healing in the hearts of many. MaryAiñe shows us the way with actual tools and techniques; may your journey be equally blessed with insight and empowerment. Brava!"

—Tobey Crockett, PhD, Teacher, change agent and activist

"In her chapter 'Waking Up Sleeping Beauty' in Sovereign Unto Herself, *Aurora Farber's evocative imagery and poetic description of her journey into her own sovereignty shine a light on the reality of so many women who grew up indoctrinated into the same fairy-tales; our limited choice between passivity and strength, the fragile frozen beauty that only hints at the glory within, and the projection of our own power onto an external 'prince' for our happily ever after. Through her tale, she paints an alternative image of happily ever after; a sisterhood of women—past, present, and future—ready to reflect each other's light to the world. With grace, warmth and whimsy, Aurora inspires us to ROAR our own truth as the powerful, divine beings that we are."*

—Rosalinde Trinnear, Designer of Open Spaces for Inspirational Living

"Taida has the heart of a gentle poet. She speaks the language of nature—of trees and flowers, of crystals and song. It is her sensitivity that provides the strength and introspection to write such a beautiful piece, 'Emanating Love Undeterred' in Sovereign Unto Herself. *As you read this piece, you're transported into her loving kindness—her ability to wrap you in hope and possibility."*

—Rebecca Cavender, Intuitive Writer

"So very often, the excavation and overcoming of pain and rebirth draw on the language of poetry to express itself. In Sovereign unto Herself, *Coco Oya does this wonderfully. She offers us a powerful, lyrical exploration of her own emergence from a place of darkness into the enlightened repossession of Self."*

—Jacob Ross, Award-winning writer, Fellow of the Royal Society of Literature

"In Sovereign Unto Herself, *Michelle Orwick expresses so many of the ideas and concepts I've started to uncover myself. The way she expresses them is filled with such love, clarity, and understanding it instantly resonates with me at a fuller level than I could have imagined. Her words show me how to embody and empower my own sovereignty in a way that just feels beautiful."*

—Lisa Toney of Infinite Resonance Therapy

"In Deborah Harlow's emotional and insightful recapturing of her own feminine journey, she gifts each of us our own opportunity for healing and growth. Her words in Sovereign Unto Herself give us the courage to find our own 'Queen Voice' while modeling how to access our own joyful YES. It is an honor to walk this path with a healer and creator who is so grounded in her own truth while lovingly illuminating the path for the collective female experience."

—Melody Gabay Pourmoradi, Founder of Life Evolutions & Girlife Empowerment

"In 'Traveling the Path of Solitude to Find My True Voice', Rina Liv's ability to be completely vulnerable and open about her painful past is absolutely phenomenal. Her journey of self discovery and her path to experiencing unconditional love through her relationship with God—and through her children—is nothing short of inspiring. Her story has encouraged and helped me to open and evaluate some hidden and painful memories of my own. Sovereign Unto Herself shows us how important it is to heal and regain our ultimate power that God has given each and everyone of us. Through God, all things really are possible and we can all live happier and healthier lives because of it."

—Briana Mussaw, The Reader's Compass, International Book Reviewers

"Elsa Perez Dean's mythic story in Sovereign Unto Herself is a deep reflection that opens a door for so many of us who have felt trapped in a life of shame and unworthiness. Her journey to her own sovereign power is courageous and uplifting. 'Reclaiming My Birthright to Sovereign Power and Joy' is a story of connection, healing, and vulnerability that speaks to the heart and lights up the Divine Mother in all of us."

—Jackie Jordan, Founder of Grounded Journeys

"In Sovereign unto Herself, Coco's account of reclaiming her sovereignty epitomizes what it means to rise like a phoenix from the ashes of a life seemingly destroyed by the painful disempowerment of a child. Her journey to re-ignite her inner fire will not fail to fan the flames of your heart— a true inspiration for anyone ready to learn what it really means to discover self-love."

—Katie Mottram, Founder of #Emerging Proud

"It touches my heart profoundly reading the chapter written by Rima Bonario from Sovereign Unto Herself. *Rima courageously reveals her personal story, sharing intimate details of her voyage to claim her sexual sovereignty. Her story is unique for her, but also universal for other women—describing how important polarity is for a couple. Most women can relate to, from time to time, being more in a* doing *than a* being *mode, being more in her head than in her body, and longing for a more fulfilling love life and more attraction! Rima gives us an example of what it takes to be more in your feminine state by trying something new outside your comfort zone. It is inspiring to read and learn from her journey!"*

—Dr. Helle Trankjær, Specialist in general medicine, family doctor, Specialist in clinical sexology and FECSM (Fellow of the European Commitee of Sexual Medicine), Chief physician at the department of sexology at Roskilde hospital in Denmark

"I was incredibly moved by Aurora Farber's chapter, 'Waking Up Sleeping Beauty in Sovereign Unto Herself. *Her ability to weave together poetry, archetypal Disney characters, and symbolic dream interpretation is a potent mix! Aurora beautifully describes her empowerment journey in this collection of writing. It is deeply personal while also being relevant to so many, and carries the strength and magic of the feminine like only women can. A treasure."*

—Flora Ware, Leadership Mentor & Sacred Business Coach, Speaker, Author, Priestess

"Taida Horozovic serves as an example and inspiration of how we can all be: in harmony with our true selves. In Sovereign Unto Herself, *this passionate priestess shows us what it means to be vulnerable. She shows us what it means to be authentic. And she shows us what can happen when we tap into our creative Source. Providing practical tips for how to turn toward our own soul's calling, Horozovic offers a window into her own inner journey. Her essay 'Emanating Love Undeterred' will leave you feeling affirmed and motivated to take your next step with intention."*

—Kathryn Maddux

FLOWER *of* LIFE PRESS

Book design by Jane Astara Ashley, floweroflifepress.com
Cover artwork by Adrianne SpiralLight

To contact the publisher, visit floweroflifepress.com

Library of Congress Control Number: Available Upon Request
Flower of Life Press, *Old Saybrook, CT.*

ISBN-13: 978-1-7349730-2-0

Printed in the United States of America

Dedication

In love and dedication to our beloved sister Adrianne SpiralLight whose artwork adorns the cover of this book. Adrianne passed away before we could receive her chapter for this book, but we did receive the art for the cover. Adrianne contributed to the fifth book in the New Feminine Evolutionary Series called, Set Sail: Shine Your Radiance, Activate Your Ascension, Ignite Your Income, Live Your Legacy. *Her essay from that book,* "Easy Joy: Remembering the 'More' of Who We Are" *is featured as a bonus chapter in this collection. Infinite gratitude, Adrianne. We love you.*

—Jane Astara Ashley, Publisher

Adrianne,

Your gifts were undeniable. Your heart was full of pure love. Your ability to tune into the divine was a powerful amplifier for anyone who was held in your presence. A gifted artist and word-smith; may your magical spirit move through us as the container for this work.

Rest in peace beloved sister.

Always your friend,
Jacquie Eva Rose, www.harmoniousbeing.co.uk

Table of Contents

Featured Authors

Contributing Authors

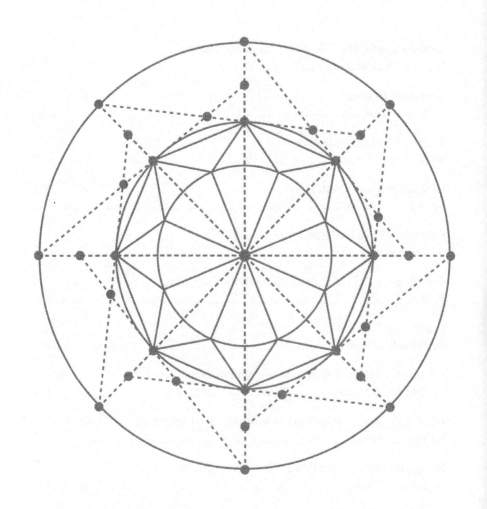

Introduction

The Call to Stand as Sovereign Queen

BY JANE ASTARA ASHLEY

A PASSING... AND AN OPENING

As I sit to write this introduction, I am reflecting on the power of life and death. Why? Because on this morning around 4:30 a.m., my 93-year-old mother-in-law Esther passed away, succumbing to the COVID-19 virus and pneumonia.

Esther certainly was a fighter; she went through so many surgeries and illnesses that I can't even keep track. She'd be on the brink of death, wind up in the hospital, and before we knew it, she'd bounce back and be as perky as ever! We thought, *if anyone can survive this, it's her.*

Esther lived with our family for three years before going into the nursing home, and as her caregiver, I witnessed her onset of dementia and how she changed over time. My husband Scott told me she had been quite a challenge in her younger years but had become more gentle and softer as she aged. She was always very pleasant with everyone, and I never saw her emotions get the best of her. She held her center just as a Sovereign Queen does, with poise, confidence, and no time for pettiness. She was also one for enjoying and celebrating life; early on, we enjoyed our nightly glass of white wine on the couch with the dog while watching "Jeopardy" together.

Almost every day from then on, Scott was over at the nursing home, visiting and tending to the other residents, consciously uplifting them and giving increase to every person over there, including the healthcare workers and families that he met. He was like an angel, dropped down into the middle of these "forgotten" elders and bed- or wheelchair-bound people, those whose bodies had served them up a plate of pain and disconnection. Scott's silly, jester-like nature would bring a smile to their faces. His gentle touch on a shoulder or direct but gentle eye contact created an instant transmission of love. Scott was Esther's biggest fan, and she was his. Theirs was a very special connection that mirrored back to me what I desire to create with my *own* mother as I support her through her aging process—how I, too, can serve with unconditional love and a pure intention.

Esther ultimately surrendered her fight and finally let go. I imagine her final release as she gently fell back into the arms of love—of Great Mother—to be held and shepherded through to the next phase of the Mystery, enveloped in bliss, love, safety, and surrounded by loved ones.

I am grateful for my mother-in-law, for she was an elder who taught me so many things about how to live and love as a Sovereign Queen—without having to say a word. Esther certainly showed me how to be a fighter and move forward with confidence no matter what gets in my way.

Scott and I have been able to release the co-dependencies that had built up over twelve years of being in partnership together. Now, we honor each other's desires and divine humanity by treating each other with the respect that a King and Queen must uphold to reign with love and compassion. Sacred sexual sovereignty and Sacred Union with my husband are only possible because we honor the balance of the masculine and feminine energies inside of ourselves first, as sovereign beings.

WHAT IT MEANS TO BE SOVEREIGN...

There is a web of codependency that operates beneath your daily awareness; the seeds of discontent and powerlessness that were planted even before you were born, generational traumas and habits passed down to you through DNA and energetic blocks.

These fears and beliefs can haunt your very existence, and most parents unwittingly reinforce them through their own stories and behavior. Anger, abuse, chemical dependencies, and social "rules" all work to build your belief system, in essence, creating a "box" that controls every decision and action—limiting success in relationships and hindering the personal evolution and connection that we seek.

By examining these co-dependencies, women can connect challenges with solutions, clearing the path toward a state of sovereignty and the freedom that the right use of power can create.

The strength of my personal relationship with Spirit has been vital in claiming my sovereignty; it has enabled me to discover the power and magic of "presence", embody my Soul, feel connected to life, and receive support from the Divine.

Perhaps your relationship with Spirit is not as strong as you'd like and you are not feeling sovereign... If so, make a commitment today to change and embody *more* of your sovereignty because, *sister, I believe in you!* You can make any change and create whatever you desire! The Divine is there to help, but only if you stop, turn to face it, ask for help, and then listen for guidance from within.

It's taken a while to integrate these pieces so that my energy body and physical body understand what Sovereignty really is, what it feels like, and why it's a necessary step on my path. Now, I know that if I am to walk through life with an open heart, ready to hold all of it with grace—the dark and the light... the cycle of life, death, and rebirth—then trust, courage, and confidence are a must.

Sovereignty is a life-long quest and requires tending as each new layer becomes revealed. When we witness each other and do this together in sisterhood, the process is enlivening and connecting.

10 TRUTHS OF EMBODIED SOVEREIGN QUEEN ENERGY

1. **A Sovereign Queen is in alignment with her truth.** She's been around and has experienced enough of life to know that it includes not just love and light, but also shadow, pain, and suffering. She's not afraid to face it all with honesty and an open heart and mind. She uses the pain in her life as fuel for strength and wisdom. She uses it to *rise* and take a stand for *truth* in order to affect change.

2. **A Sovereign Queen knows and trusts herself.** She's done the work and no longer looks outside of herself for validation. She does not people-please or have a need for people to like or approve of her. Instead, she holds compassion and fierce love for herself and her own boundaries, as well as for those around her grid. She holds no self-judgment and, therefore, does not judge anyone else, either.

3. **A Sovereign Queen is a daughter of the Divine.** She knows that her role is to simply be herself without any masks—and that this is enough. She knows she is *not* broken, that there is nothing wrong with her, nothing missing, nothing to fix. She is complete and lives in a state of integrated wholeness. She is in touch with her own nobility as a Divine child and carries forth an authentic, regal nature.

4. **A Sovereign Queen rides with the punches goes with the flow, and laughs her ass off through all if it.** She knows that her power and her words matter. She knows that her energy ripples out and affects change and creates transformation, so she is benevolent with her power and willing to constantly look at and transmute any lurking shadows or lower energies.

5. **A Sovereign Queen exudes love, truth, and compassion,** but is not afraid to access her fierce, "burn-that-shit-down" swiftness when it comes to alchemizing anything less than love back to love.

6. **A Sovereign Queen knows she is supported by her team of guides in the physical, spiritual, and energetic realms.** She is no longer the lone wolf having to do it all herself. Instead, she honors synarchy and the joy of working together in unity and harmony for the good of the collective, like bees in a hive.

7. **A Sovereign Queen is willing to heed the call toward leadership.** She takes action to serve her inner circle, her community, and the collective with her sacred assignment on the planet.

8. **A Sovereign Queen activates her Creatrix energy.** She seeks New Earth solutions and dreaming into emergence new possibilities, modalities, structures, and systems that serve the collective. She activates the law of "As Above, So Below," by dreaming and visualizing her desires, then takes action to manifest them by pulling spirit down into three-dimensional form. She is detached from the outcome and completely surrendered to the Divine. She is willing to let go of anything that isn't working, try something new, and innovative.

9. **A Sovereign Queen sees "life as the initiation."** She trusts that life is not happening *to* her, but *for* her.

10. **A Sovereign Queen checks her ego at the door.** She asks herself, "Is this intention, action, or creation in service to the collective, or in service to my ego?" If it's ego-based, she drops it like a hot potato.

Sister, are you ready to claim your power and your birthright as the Sovereign Queen of your Queendom?

The authors in this book are ready; and I am so pleased to share their wisdom with you. The stories, tools, and resources that they share will elevate your life and bring increase to you and those around you... as you RISE into your Sovereign Queen with the utmost grace... and hilarity!

When you are sovereign, you and your power become One.

When you are sovereign, your choices reflect your higher power.

When you are sovereign, relationships are balanced instead of codependent.

When you are sovereign, you take responsibility for yourself and your actions without blame or judgment.

When you are sovereign, you trust your intuition.

When you are sovereign, the doorway to abundance swings wide open.

—*Astara, Publisher of Flower of Life Press*

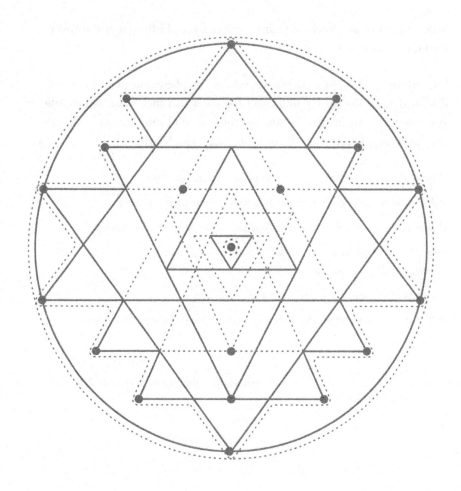

Sexual Sovereignty:
Tapping into the Power of Pleasure

BY RIMA BONARIO, TH.D

My husband sat across from me on the bed after yet another failed attempt at sexual intimacy. My body had been closed, as usual, and his patience was thin.

This was a painful pattern we had been trapped in for eleven years, ever since the birth of our daughter. I didn't understand it. I loved my husband deeply. I was attracted to him (he's hot!). And I longed for a juicy and fulfilling sex life. But ever since the blush of early romance had been replaced by the pull of raising a child and running two businesses, our sex life had sucked.

"I want you to fix this," he said in a moment of brutal honesty.

At the time, we both believed that it was my problem. Of course, we later came to see it was a joint problem stemming from our inability to keep the polarity strong in our relationship. But more on that later.

In response to his request, I began scouring the internet for help. I wasn't looking for the usual help of sex therapists or self-help books that said I should just dress up and be more sexy. I had proved in my college days that I knew how to have sex—lots of it. But that didn't necessarily lead to intimacy. And I knew my issues went deep. They likely had their roots in my Catholic upbringing and a history of not feeling safe.

I came across the book *Red Hot & Holy: A Heretic's Love Story* by Sera Beak. And then I heard her speak. She was tracking something entirely new to me—a way of being that was deeply feminine and at the same time unapologetically powerful, authentic, and edgy.

I signed up for her week-long SoulFire retreat and began my journey to reclaim my sexual sovereignty.

Sexual sovereignty for me was about claiming my right to be a sexual being—on my own terms. Maybe that's a no-brainer for some people. But it wasn't for me. My desire, my sexual power, my turn-on was mostly lost to me in my day-to-day life. I could gain access to it sometimes if I had a couple of glasses of wine. Or, before I was married, there was a ton of it when meeting a new lover. But it never lasted.

My husband, like most men, could easily get to his turn-on. Unfortunately for me, he was, and still is not, much of a romantic. His style of flirting has always been a bit off-putting to me—a kind of adolescent humor that leans toward dirty. He was short of compliments and easily frustrated in the bedroom with having to "warm me up" all the time. Not at all what got me going.

But once I *did* get going, things were generally good. He was and is a caring lover—albeit, in the beginning not a skilled one.

My hunt for help led me to study energy work with Linda Caesara and Tj Bartel, and to later go on to study and practice Tantra with Tj. At a 10-day deep dive workshop, Linda and Tj radically changed my understanding of how my body works. It was like they pulled back the curtain on the mystery of me and suddenly everything made sense.

Here's some of what I learned:

- A woman's energy body functions differently from a man's.
- We all have both masculine and feminine energy.
- Heterosexual couples will become depolarized if the woman runs too much masculine energy (doing and giving) and the man runs too much feminine energy (receiving and stillness).
- Women are energized by receiving and drained by giving, whereas men are the opposite.
- We want and need to operate out of both poles in our body, but, especially in the bedroom, women should receive more and men should give more.

- A woman's body may need up to 45 minutes to properly warm up to have a full orgasmic experience.
- Too many clitoral orgasms leave a woman's energy system dried out.

As it turns out, I was operating almost exclusively out of my masculine energy. As a go-getter entrepreneur and proud wife and mom, I had so much of my life firing on all cylinders. I ran a successful business, raised a thriving and busy child, enjoyed fulfilling friendships, and had a beautiful home... but the cost of making all that happen was my feminine essence.

I knew how I got there, how I rejected my feminine essence. I remember it like it was yesterday. I was eleven and growing into a woman. With my dad running the show, my mother was deeply disempowered. To me, she seemed weak, forever giving up on her positions, on herself, and on us kids—failing to protect us from my dad's wrath (or her own).

And then along came Enjouli, and the perfume commercial that cemented my separation from my feminine.

"I can bring home the bacon,
fry it up in a pan,
and never, never, never let you forget you're a man!
Cause I'm a woman!
Enjouli"

There it was! The recipe for being a successful woman!

And off I went, convinced I had to do and be it *all* to be desirable and worthy. I fell into a pattern of striving to be exceptionally competent in all I did and failing to take care of myself or even notice my own needs. By always doing, doing, doing, I had unknowingly shut down and dulled my pleasure receptors. Sex had become a chore, something to endure, another "to do" in being a good wife.

For us as a heterosexual couple, this was bad news.

I learned that running my energy in this way meant that, energetically speaking, there were two masculine energies in the bed. We repelled each other instead of magnetizing each other. It's like we were trying to bring the same poles of two magnets together. What I needed was to shift deeply into my feminine essence so that our relationship could be more polarized.

Linda and Tj explained that I needed to turn up the volume on my feminine energy so that I could unleash the fabulous, feisty, and fun parts of myself.

I asked my husband for his blessing to do hands-on work with Tj. That meant hiring him to serve as my Daka, to awaken my sexual energy. This was very edgy and super scary. My husband agreed, but with some limitations. He knew the work meant I would be naked and Tj would touch me. My husband said as long there was no penetration of any kind it was fine.

Tj and I scheduled the first session. I had no idea what to expect. Tj gently explained the ways Tantric massage can turn on a woman's body and help awaken and connect circuitry and pleasure centers in my brain. He talked about dopamine, serotonin, phenylalanine, and other hormones that my brain would produce as he massaged my body. He said it wouldn't be like therapeutic massage but more like an erotic massage. I swallowed hard. After I disrobed and laid face down on the bed, he returned and began the massage.

As he worked to help me relax, my body began to respond. I started breathing deeply and with each breath I came more fully into my body. What I found there shocked me.

I was EXHAUSTED! Not just tired, but BONE-TIRED.

As I felt into the exhaustion, and at the same time felt the warmth and love flowing from Tj's hands, I began to cry, and then to sob. He encouraged me to let the tears flow. His gentle voice reassuring me that all was well. I cried and cried until I had no more tears.

Then it was time to turn over. He continued massaging me. He expertly stroked my belly, my breasts, and my thighs, waking up my body to the pleasure it could feel. It took me an hour to open my eyes. And when I did, he was right there, waiting for me. It took my breath away!

I had never felt so much love being poured into me. Of course, he explained that this was the hormones activating the pleasure receptors, but it was also his skill, and his loving heart.

That session ended and I knew I wanted and needed more. I wanted to become fully orgasmic. And I had no doubt he could help me. I knew it would likely take many sessions. And I knew I had to get my husband's buy-in. Grudgingly yet courageously facing his own fears, he agreed.

Over the course of the next few months, my husband made space for me to fly to California to work with Tj, while he stayed at home processing his fear, grief, and anger. It wasn't easy to stay the course. We made mistakes. We had botched communications that caused pain. And waves of profound fear. More than once we discussed whether we should divorce so I could continue this work on my own. But the thing was, I had absolutely no desire to leave my marriage.

It was utterly meaningless to explore my sexuality as a single woman; it was hugely important to own my right to explore my sexuality in this way *within the commitment of my relationship.* I needed to find and reclaim my sexual sovereignty while still deeply committed to my relationship. I needed my husband to be able to hold that—to know our commitment was as strong as ever and it could make room for this exploration.

Not surprisingly, the work began paying off almost immediately. We went from attempting intimacy once a month to two to four times a week. And in most cases the experience was positive. Again, it wasn't easy.

Eventually, the three of us began to work together. And it was a game changer!

I'm so lucky. My amazing husband is nothing if not dedicated to his growth. He leaned in deeply, learning all he could from Tj about deepening his own masculine energy, about how to give with his touch rather than take, and how to bring my body into new levels of pleasure.

He was so taken by the experience of watching me bloom that he decided to become a Daka himself! Now he's certified to help other women awaken their pleasure centers and relax into their sexual power.

Most if not all of our squabbles have disappeared because the power struggles that marked our marriage were a symptom of our mismatched polarity. Things flow more easily between us now, and we often wonder what it was we used to argue about.

We are still human and still have to work at our marriage, but the dream we had of creating a fulfilling and juicy sex life has come true.

Just as important is the knowing that I am no longer bound by old patriarchal ideas about what I can and can't do with my body. Gone is the confusion about pleasure and sexual communion; I now see them as sacred and holy rites that unlock doorways into higher levels of consciousness, and I get to experience that regularly.

Sound too *woo woo* for you? All I can say, sister, is try it.

You owe it to yourself. And the world needs you deeply accessing your power. All of it!

Special Gifts

Dr. Rima Bonario has two special free gifts to assist you in exploring your self-sovereignty.

Visit **www.thesevenqueendoms.com** to download a one-page guide to the Seven Queendoms of Self-Sovereignty. This guide introduces you to the seven queen archetypes and the essential oils, elements, gemstones and more that will help you activate these Queendoms in your life.

Visit **www.7daystoawaken.com** for a potent, seven-day mini-course that will allow you to awaken your sexual and life-force energy in just 5-7 minutes a day! Get ready to feel more alive than ever before!

Dr. Rima Bonario is a Dream Weaver, Soul-Coach and Wild-Heart Healer. Through her workshops, classes, transformational travel journeys, and private coaching, she helps women shift out of fear and frustration into a life they love.

Rima speaks and teaches on personal sovereignty and the challenge many women face in maintaining a healthy balance between caring for others and caring for ourselves. She weaves together a safe and sacred place to explore the healing power of myths and archetypes, ritual and ceremony, and Soul/shadow work to re-pattern and resolve childhood conditioning.

Rima is the founder of the Sisterhood of Anointing Priestesses where she explores and initiates lost Temple Arts. One of Rima's greatest loves is growing her Travel Sangha by leading sacred pilgrimages to spiritually potent locations such as Egypt, Hawaii, Southern France, and soon the British Isles.

Rima is published author and a four-time contributor to the New Feminine Evolutionary Series from Flower of Life Press. She is also the co-author of the beautiful full-color book *Who Have you Come Here to BE? 101 Possibilities for Contemplation* and the companion twin card decks.

Rima earned her doctorate in Transformational Psychology from Holos University Graduate Seminary. She currently studies Egyptian Anointing Mysteries with Gamal Abdul, Energy Work and Tantra Embodiment with Tj Bartel, Mystical Mindset with Halle Eavelyn, and Energy Shamanism with Trevor Hart. Her other mentors include Soul-Whisperer Sera Beak, Master Energy Teacher Lynda Caesara, and Tantric Masters Charles Muir and Mantak Chia.

Learn more at **RimaBonario.com.**

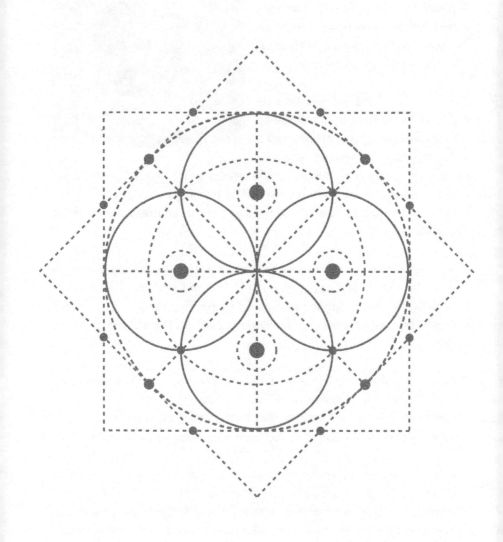

Artist Ascension: Four Pillars to Activate Your Sacred Work and Birth a New Earth

BY ALEXIS COHEN

PART I—THE VISION

Artists are channels, bringing the world of the unseen into the seen.

> "This is for YOU. The one that is listening. You're being called into the LIGHT, into service that's larger than yourself, into the process of remembering who you are and why you are here. You're an Artist of the New Earth. We are here for you, and it's time to listen."
>
> —COUNCIL OF LIGHT

I'm very aware of the little voice chirping in the background. *Alexis—are you really going to put all this in print?*

Yep. It's a "Coming out of the Spiritual Closet" kind of moment. Artists are channels, bringing the world of the unseen into the seen. My creative calling is bigger than the fear and worry of what you'll think of me.

That's how I define Sovereignty: remembering, embodying, and taking action on a Sacred Assignment. There is massive freedom in taking a stand.

I know there are more of you out there. *Ones like me*—Creative Channels, Visionaries, Change Makers, Artists of Ascension. We are waking up to who we are—and claiming our *Sovereign Power.*

Like any transformational process, the road can get bumpy. Mine certainly did! So this is me—putting it into print—my story and how I learned to connect with *creative sovereign power.* This message is in service to supporting you in *creating a pathway* to your own Ascension process—one filled with ease, flow, and joy.

The first time I met the Council of Light, I was driving home from a transformational workshop.

It hit me like a ton of bricks. Something was out of alignment. And here's what became clear: one of the biggest priorities in my life is that I am an ARTIST with a big vision. But the artwork I was creating felt dry and uninspiring. Flat. And up until that moment, *I had no idea how to access that BIG VISION.*

Let me rewind. Earlier that day—in the workshop—as I turned my heart inside out to discover *what I really, truly want,* I surprised myself by declaring, "I will create a large multimedia show. With poetry, music, dance, film—and *me*—in front of a big audience."

WHAT?!?? The words spilled right from my lips, before I could gather them up or get in the way. It was *declared.* I was doing a show—and didn't have the first clue how.

Now, it's the drive home, and I'm excited, wrung out, peaceful. Open to the possibilities lying ahead of me. *And then it happened...*

Before my very eyes, the landscape changed—suddenly the Southern California hills and freeways that *should be there* were replaced by a future city, filled with otherworldly cars, buildings, and lights from 2000 years into the future. And yet... it was *familiar.*

A spiritual opening was happening while I was driving. It was so intense that I began to pull over, and then I heard a voice, clear as day, "Keep driving. Move into it. Drive into the future."

I had been a shamanic practitioner for more than 15 years, and I have always loved those moments when the veil between this world and the world of Spirit grew thin. But this was like nothing else I had experienced!

I kept driving... moving into it... *into the future.*

I listened to those voices as they unfolded beauty, vision, art, and wisdom. I was being introduced to new collaborators, new guidance—and my life has never been the same.

These allies in the Spirit World—*The Council of Light*—are here to support the transformation occurring on the planet right now. Call them Spirit Guides, Angels, God, Source, the Divine... whatever works for you!

> *The opportunity is to* listen. *And then to* create *through committed actions.*

The Council of Light has been my main collaborator in the Spirit World ever since that moment. They taught me how to activate my creative mission. They brought me home to myself as an Artist of Ascension. They encouraged me. They supported me to be of service, and to step beyond myself in order to create as a channel of higher frequencies.

And we made a pretty awesome multimedia show together! *The Butterfly People & the Dreaming Tree.* Filled with poetry, music, dance, film—and *me*—in front of a big audience. And it was wondrous.

Spirit is calling.

Spirit is calling out to the artists, healers, and change-makers who are ready to listen.

Saying YES to being a giant Channel of Light and LOVE on the planet and creating Art in collaboration with the Divine... I mean... *come on!* Is there any better way to contribute?

This path isn't alway easy or comfortable. But, honestly, I've never experienced anything more rewarding. It's what I'm here to do.

So. What is it that you *really, truly want?*

> "You are ready to be born into the light and spread the Wings that you have forgotten. It is time to reclaim your throne, restore the temples, and step into YOUR SOVEREIGNTY."
>
> *–COUNCIL OF LIGHT*

You've come to the planet with your sacred mission. As a sovereign being, empowered and aligned, you're spreading wings and taking flight. Think of the Council of Light as your flight attendants. You're the ground crew. You work together. Stay connected to them, and you'll stay connected to your mission.

The next "part" of this chapter is filled with their channeled messages, punctuated with some of my own experiences. The teachings from the Council of Light is what I hear when I tune into their guidance on how to come into alignment as a Creative Channel, work in collaboration with Spirit, and bring forward high-frequency bodies of work that support the birth of the New Earth.

This is Artist Ascension. It's a transformational process—and guidance for developing yourself as a channel of the New Earth and birthing a sacred body of work.

In the Artist Ascension Process, there are four main *Pillars,* or doorways you will pass through to release old programming and come into alignment with yourself as a channel.

Let go of any ideas about it being a linear process. It's not! That took some getting used to for me. But, once I let go, it was familiar. So, let's let go! Let's step into the non-linear. Into flow. It's ever-evolving. It's cyclical. As you step into more creative power, you will find yourself circling back to revisit these Pillars.

Each cycle is another opportunity to reach new levels, new insight, and new power.

PART II—THE ACTION

Pillar 1: Restoring Your Relationship with the Divine Feminine and Sacred Masculine

> "The Divine Feminine and the Christ Conscious-ness meet through your instruments. Spirit and Matter. They hold the energy, the frequency of healing and transformation."
>
> *–COUNCIL OF LIGHT*

You are in a birthing space. Time works differently here.

Living day to day, it's obvious that we are body. But we're also spirit. We are here and now, on this beautiful Earth, and... we're everywhere. This world seems to be composed of opposites and contradictions. I'm interested in building bridges. *Beautiful bridges.*

When I first starting dipping into all this, it hit me–

I'm a Jewish lady. Is it okay that I talk to Jesus?

I was born Jewish, and I always felt like I didn't belong. I started Hebrew school late. I always felt behind, stupid. I didn't understand the rituals. And *it didn't grab me.* I knew I was a spiritual person, but I wasn't feeling that *spark*, that energizing sense of home.

I tried a few times as a young adult to jump-start my connection to Judaism. I felt the cultural connection. But that was it. There seemed to be nowhere for my spirituality to *ground*.

Then I learned about the Great Mother and the Divine Feminine.

And there was the *SPARK!*

In my late twenties, I discovered circles of women in the San Francisco Bay Area studying shamanic tools and techniques and earth-based wisdom. I learned about birthing babies and the creative force that flows through it.

In connecting with the Divine Feminine, I found my voice. I found spirituality and power. I found that spiritual home where I could ground and make that connection between body and spirit.

I supported birthing women as a doula and supported three hundred new lives coming Earthside. The Divine Feminine was everywhere in my life. I was surrounded by women, inspired by women, and supporting women.

So just when I've got it all dialed in, who waltzed into my shamanic journeys?

Jesus.

And not as a walk-on role. He wasn't making a cameo; he was showing up as my *main* guide of Ascension.

He showed up with a gift greater than those Christmas packages I'd missed out on a kid: Christ Consciousness. Sacred Masculinity. The Healing Balm. The Generous King. The Loving Brother. The Ascended Artist. The masculine who just *loves* collaboration with the feminine.

The Divine Feminine and Sacred Masculine work together in the Ascension Process. The Great Mother and the Earth anchor the high frequencies of Christ Consciousness.

When you connect to your sovereign Divine Feminine Nature, you open and receive. You connect to the Earth. The Great Mother guides and catalyzes this transformational, creative processes—for you and the whole planet.

The Sacred Masculine and Christ Consciousness energies flood onto our planet as high-frequency love and light. It's brilliant. Renewing. Unifying. It's the sun on your face. It's the fire that builds stars. Call it whatever you want. It doesn't belong to a particular religion or sect. It's for all of us.

I pushed it away for a while. *I'm Jewish. I study Buddhism. I revere the Great Mother... This isn't for me.*

But it is time to break down all of those walls that keep us divided.

It's time to go underneath the structures and identities that have held us back and separate.

ALL of the Divine—the feminine and masculine aspects of light and love— are ready to work in harmony through YOU.

And there *will* be presents!

Pillar 2: Restoring Connection and A Deep Relationship To Your Body

> "Your sweet body doesn't lie. You have in your possession the body of truth—it holds the memories, the stories, and the blueprint to your creative mission."
>
> *-COUNCIL OF LIGHT*

Sugar. *Why must you act so sweet?* For years I numbed my body with sugar and stuffed all my feelings down with food so I didn't have to feel the pain.

Again, things changed and healing became possible when I decided to *listen.* Once I was willing to face the trauma and grief stored in my body, a direct line to my guidance opened up.

When I rush or move too quickly, it's hard to hear my body's sweet wisdom. When I'm brave and kind enough to listen to her, to stay close in every moment, all day long, I hear the answer. What a gift! This is what I hear: the natural, harmonious sound of body connected to spirit.

We've all heard it before: Your body is your temple.

But let's say it again. Slowly. Thoughtfully. Tune in, and listen:

Your *body is your temple.*

Imprinted on her walls are the codes and blueprints of her mission. We have the gift, the privilege, and the responsibility to *restore the temple.*

This is about going deeper, listening deeper, and connecting to all the layers of stored wisdom within us. Connecting to our sparkling, activated DNA, to the light codes that form our structure and create our bodies with the brilliant light of wisdom.

The Ascension Process is an embodied process. Our bodies have all the information we need to connect to the world of energy and spirit. Within us are the codes that allow us to awaken to our true selves, to tune in, and to create and restore those unifying, *beautiful bridges* for the world.

Pillar 3: Restoring Connection To Sacred Art

"It is your responsibility as humans to remember, discover, and develop your gifts. All good teachers help you to remember. No one 'knows' more than anyone else. You are all one."

-COUNCIL OF LIGHT

Creating art is a Spiritual practice for me. It took awhile for me to take that stand and say it confidently. But now it's a simple truth. The canvas or page is the meeting place, the connection point between the world of the seen and the unseen. When I create Sacred Art in collaboration with the Divine, I go right to the Source of who I am. It's like I open up the door and unlock the code of my remembering.

Artists of this time are being called forward to travel into the depths of the world of the unseen and bring back the wisdom, the healing, and the visions for the greater community. In this time, that community is a global one. As Artists of the New Earth, our connection to Spirit needs to be solid and clear. We are being called to bravely step into Sovereign Power and use our creative voices. Loudly. Boldly!

Artists are leaders, riding at the forefront of shifts in our global consciousness. As a sovereign feminine leader, we light the way from a place of fierce compassion and love.

Sacred Art is evolving. As we enter the next Golden Era—one dripping in the Divine Nectar that bridges ancient and new ways of creating—we are called to tune into the high frequencies coming through and to create new blueprints and maps of the Earth through art.

The work at the forefront of changing times holds the frequencies of transcendence and transformation. Above all else, those high frequencies of light and consciousness support the masses in transcending and transforming lower frequencies.

Those lower frequencies that sweet-talk us into stasis and sleep can create a fog of collective amnesia. Sacred Art is a brilliant shout to WAKE UP, move forward—and *create!*

Pillar 4: Restoring Connection To Your Treasury

"When you work with us on a regular basis, your commitment to these collaborations with Spirit and the Council of Light deepens and grows, and your creative missions, projects, and creations will be bigger and require more resources."

-COUNCIL OF LIGHT

"I can't afford it."

When I first moved to Los Angeles, I was broke. Like, *painfully* broke. I had left the San Francisco community in which I thrived for over a decade. I was starting from scratch. That first year in LA was hard, scraping together rent through healing gigs and sporadic workshops and circles. My life was not matching the vision that I *knew* I came to LA to birth.

Then I met a new mentor, and things shifted. New ideas. New callings. Opportunities I knew *I just had to experience!* I knew I needed to work with this mentor. But that's a big new expense every month! *How am I going to pay for it?* First things first: I took the leap and said YES.

And something completely shifted. I activated a new level of trust and belief in myself. I had the determination to show up *committed* to my vision, and the money started to flow in. First a little at a time, then in consistently larger amounts.

We have a lot of money stories to transform within the artistic and healing communities. The romanticism of the struggling artist and the vows of poverty that span lifetimes–that's thick karma to break up. But *we've gotta do it.*

We have big visions. Big Visions come from Big Power. We can connect to that source.

Your mission is funded already. Unlock the treasury that exists in the energetic world. It involves listening, connecting, committing, and saying YES. You will be given what you need depending on where you are in the mission.

This is a paradigm shift. This isn't waiting and praying for money to come before you act on the dream in your heart. It's a leap of faith, followed by Committed Action. Take action—and then resources will flow behind it. Wealth wants a channel in order to flow in. *Action* and *commitment* unlock a wealth channel. The money needs you to stretch, it needs the space to come in.

When you say YES to your creative mission, your life reorganizes around you. When you align with your guidance and vision, you generate commitment. When you show up, take action, and continue to say YES, you generate results. And you take your place as an Artist of Ascension, transforming this global community and creating the New Earth!

PART III–THE CALLING

On that drive home, with those familiar Southern California hills replaced by a vision of the future, I wanted to panic. I wanted to pull over the car.

Instead, I listened.

I kept driving, moving into it... into the future. Onto the stage, swaying and singing, collaborating with the Council of Light, surrounded by artists that I admired, collectively channeling beauty and wisdom and sharing it with my community.

I had created something bigger than I ever imagined possible. Days after the show, stories streamed in about how the show impacted the audience. There were some life-changing stories!

And that was just the beginning.

There is incredible power in completion. When you commit and keep your word, you will see yourself differently. You will be known to yourself and your guidance as a capable and trustworthy creative channel. When you continue to show up for Spirit and your creative work, you will feel worthy to continue to receive these higher frequency visions.

And when you create Sacred Art that is bigger than yourself, you create the New Earth.

This is the next level. As an Artist of Ascension, you are being called to do your inner and outer work. You are being called to heal and strengthen. You are being called to be a channel who brings through higher frequency visions and births the New Earth that will sustain us all.

It's a celebratory time! And it requires your deep commitment to your path.

And so, this chapter is dedicated to the unconditional love and guidance of the Council of Light—and to YOU! I have a feeling you are being called!

May these words inspire you to remember who you are and why you are here. May they rouse you to connect with Sovereign Power, collaborate with Spirit, and trust that you are supported. And may they activate the bravery within you to say what you think, feel and believe. Even—and especially—if it's out of this world. Listen to the call and make your ART!

Alexis Cohen is the founder of Artist Ascension Academy and Art Medicine, LLC. She a visionary artist and creativity mentor. She is also a shamanic practitioner and healer practicing for over 15 years. She has a BA in Creative Writing from San Francisco State, and studied painting and drawing at the Art Academy and Center for Creative Exploration—both schools are in San Francisco.

She received her Shamanic and hypnotherapy certifications at Foundation of the Sacred Stream in Berkeley and ran a thriving Depth Hypnosis practice for 10 years. Depth Hypnosis is a healing modality that combines Shamanism, Transpersonal Psychology, hypnotherapy and Tibetan Buddhist Psychology.

She also supported 300 new souls entering the world during her decade long career as a birth doula!

Learn more at **AlexisCohen.org.**

Special Gift

A GUIDED SHAMANIC JOURNEY
TO YOUR FEMININE POWER

Access here:
https://artmedicine.us/a-guided-shamanic-journey-to-your-feminine-power/

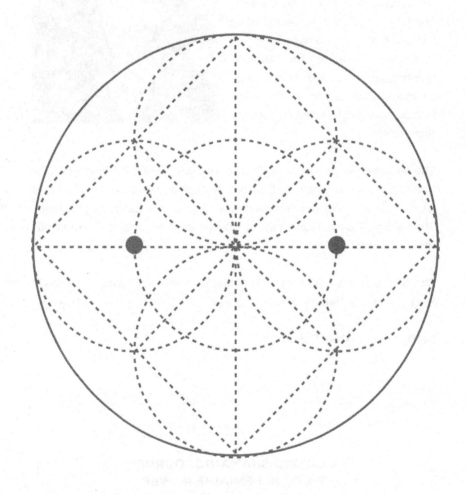

Mother Bear Is the Sovereign Queen

BY MARYAIÑE CURTIS

> "We need to accept that we won't always make
> the right decisions, that we'll screw up royally
> sometimes—understanding that failure is not
> the opposite of success, it's part of success."
>
> —ARIANNA HUFFINGTON

Signs of hope are everywhere. The caterpillar in my garden that ate voraciously until it was time to create its cocoon didn't know it would emerge with wings—until it did. The oak tree growing in the crack of a huge boulder thrived there despite the seemingly poor conditions. If these creatures can move forward without knowing what comes next, so can we.

Sovereignty begins inside. Until I was eight, I was a practicing "good girl." Then one day, a terrible thing happened that changed my life forever—an older altar boy stole my virginity. How could I know it wasn't my fault? I saw myself as damaged goods, no longer eligible to be the virgin, princess, Catholic bride. Deeply wounded and angry, I stopped believing in the authorities of my girlhood and slowly stepped into full rebellion. As a child of the sixties, this manifested in sex, drugs and rock and roll. I started drinking to fit in, skipped school, and didn't come home at night.

Even in full rebellion, I maintained hope. I took on the role of a tomboy, hanging out with my brothers, becoming a rough, tough, and very capable country girl. I served as a peer counselor in the afternoon, and worked for a dentist after school. The church condoned the Vietnam war and two of my older brothers were there at the same time. I left the church. Instead of sitting in the pews quietly with my discontent, I took action, participating in peace rallies. Despite the damage, I took charge, and decided to remain optimistic and hopeful.

........⌾⧲⌾........

Consider the possibility that we are spirit beings coming to Earth to have a human experience. We make agreements to meet at certain times through-out our life with specific spirits that will be instrumental in the growth of our souls. With these other spirits we craft a life experience that will provide the lessons we need.

My soul wanted to learn forgiveness. I made agreements with many spirits to come into my life and give me the experiences that could lead me to this les-son. Mom's deep depression when I was a baby taught me to be independent and to be strong for her. That boy who stole my virginity when I was eight taught me not to trust the guys when I was a teen. The girls of my childhood taught me that cliques were miserable and that girls were not to be trusted. My biggest contract, however, was with my true love, my knight in shining armor, my former Marine husband. I felt safe with him. He was also the one to hurt me the deepest. But through this hurt and grief, I learned and began to practice my life purpose: sovereignty and forgiveness.

Next, I'll share several examples of how sovereignty becomes a fierce focus with a call to action.

> *As I gain access to my heart and soul, I reach for the message of*
> *the sovereign Queen. She reminds me of times when I unleashed*
> *the power of my convictions in the face of patriarchal dictates.*

........⌾⧲⌾........

The Sovereign Queen inside of me lies dormant for long periods of time in my life when I don't have a cause to stand up for or someone who I need to protect. I forget that I need her myself. When the time comes to speak truth to power or to protect the unprotected, she emerges with a fierce determination to correct and shift the prevailing perception and situation. My Sovereign Queen has a voice, and she means business. When I step into my sovereignty, I move mountains. The ferocity of a mother bear comes into me, and I have such immense energy that I can advocate effectively and be heard in a good way.

Throughout my lifetime I have wavered between the cruel joke of being a martyr or a victim—all part of my matriarchal inheritance. I was unheard and invisible. I spent years doing life "his" way, following "his" rules, going along with what seemed to be okay, and justifying unacceptable behavior and brainwashing. My inner conviction and strong voice for what was right and needed to be done was always within me, though I caught only glimpses of her in my younger years. Finally, as the consequences of my choices became enormous, I stepped fully into my Sovereign Queen and came to know Her. The following vignettes include circumstances from three phases of my life where my sovereignty guided my actions.

MAIDENHOOD

It was 40-degree weather and I was a high school student. Mini skirts were the fad, but I wore a long warm dress. It was a practical, even responsible choice, but the principal punished me for violating the dress code. The hypocrisy of male authority angered me, so I spoke out to the entire school board and explained my concern for the girls in dresses. Through stepping into my sovereignty and embodying my Sovereign Queen, I achieved a change in the dress code. We could wear pants now.

MOTHERHOOD

As a young, pregnant wife, I believed that my husband couldn't be my enemy. I hoped things would get better when his construction injury healed. I stayed because I believed in marriage. I couldn't leave because I knew he was depressed. I *believed* his lies, brainwashing, and threats that he'd steal the children and I'd never see them again. I was under his control except for a small voice that knew he was crazy and dangerous. I was the last to admit how abused I was, and I had to call out his bluff. I worked at the State preschool and was mandated by law to report cases of neglect and abuse. I was terrified daily that we would be reported and the children taken because of the horrible yelling and fights in my home.

Finally, I reached a state that Alcoholics Anonymous calls "incomprehensible demoralization." I had just pulled our family out of homelessness. With the help of a women's shelter, I left my relationship long enough to secure a job and a studio. But I had to go back to my husband's terrible psychosis and addictions to rescue my children. I knew I wasn't innocent—*who is?*—but I had to focus on being a buffer between the kids and their dad until I found a way to get us *all* out.

Friday, June 30, 1989. He had left with the kids in our van earlier in the evening but hadn't returned. Where were my children? Where was their father? Terrified, I searched until midnight.

The next morning I heard that my children and their father were in a car accident. He was drunk driving. The wrecking yard let me get my purse, keys, and other belongings from the totaled van. Child Protective Services had my children in custody, and their father was in jail. I'd never felt so lost and powerless. The weekend felt like years until Monday when I could get answers and finally see my traumatized children.

On Monday, I went to the county court arraignment to see the children, and I tried to figure out why the station wagon shimmied in the front going over the grade.

Tuesday, July 4, loomed like a day of delay. But I did what I could and found an apartment.

The next day was children's court and a supervised visit. Oh my God, my babies! They looked okay, and they wanted to come home. I felt such relief, gratitude, and shame, but there was no time for victimhood.

Until that time, I'd been powerless. But with my husband safely in jail, I began moving mountains. Divine intervention gave me the opportunity for which I had prayed. I got the apartment in my name, but still needed to get the utilities turned on. The car still shimmied, but neither I nor the mechanic could find the source. I reminded myself to take one step at a time, stay sober, and get the kids free and home. I would go to Al-anon.

Thursday, I visited with the kids... they hated the food in the shelter and they were afraid. They were also worried about their dad. I assured them we're going to be fine; we have a new home, the landlord is letting me work off the deposit, and it's close to school and Grandma and Grandpa's.

Friday, July 7, a week after the accident, I started the day at Court. The children were placed into my sole custody with warnings to avoid arguing, violence, alcohol, and drugs or this order would be rescinded. Therapy was strongly suggested.

I was so grateful and happy. The car still shimmied, so I took the long way home over a gentler mountain pass with my precious cargo. I wouldn't put the kids in harm's way ever again.

At the Circle K we stopped to use the payphone, call the utility company and take in the deposit. I checked the front tire one more time. My God, there was a hole the size of an egg with steel belts breaking through the front left tire! I felt truly held on this divine mission.

My Sovereign Queen didn't have a name then except Mother Bear. She held me in empowered grace, determination, and honesty in the courtrooms the whole time.

These are the deepest scars from my life before I learned forgiveness, love, understanding, and compassion. My failures and triumphs were my initiation into adulthood. It took me growing up and being accountable to soften the shame I felt. There was no time to wallow in shame or self-pity; I had to thrive and embody the Warrior Queen Mama. I started over as a sovereign single mother. Slowly and purposely, I took my life back, went to daily meetings and weekly therapy. I worked at the zoo and took the kids with me. We rode bicycles almost everywhere. They learned as I learned how to manage PTSD so that we could practice living without the cycle of violence.

CRONEHOOD

Thirty years later. 2019. It was the last day of my solo pilgrimage to sacred sites where Mary Magdalene lived in Southern France. I was traveling on a luxurious train until a gruesome accident happened. I witnessed it from my window and was shaken by the vivid experience. But I thank my Virgo nature for being especially calm during times of crisis. The accident caused a long delay and I missed my connection. I was put on a family train to Paris with at least ten young children wildly running about for hours. They were actually life-affirming and comforting in their freedom on this less luxurious train. We were on a long trip without a meal or enough water. With the help of Google translate, the train clerk did the best he could to get me to Paris by morning.

The train finally pulled into the Paris airport at about 10:30 p.m. Exhausted, hungry, and parched beyond belief, I saw no one at the station. Hauling my luggage the best I could, I began to trudge up the long flight of stairs, aware that anyone's first impression of me would be an old disheveled woman struggling with her burden. In my fatigue, my PTSD welled up as I realized the airport was nearly vacant. "Oh my God, there's no one here to help me," I thought to myself. "And here I am, looking like a vulnerable old bag lady." I dropped my bags right there on the steps. I was totally alone, struggling to keep my mind's fear at bay. It was vital to keep my shit together until I found a room to sleep in, but I was beginning to crack. I had a choice: Look like someone ripe for victimization or take hold of myself.

Thankfully, I remembered the mudra for empty presence to help me get centered. I breathed deeply and cast my eyes back and forth to connect both hemispheres of my brain so I could think clearly. I remembered the benevolent Queen. I envisioned her elegant, stable power as I pulled myself up straight. I held my head higher and pulled my shoulders back. I took deep breaths as I pulled my auric field tight around me. I thought to myself, "If I am going to be walking through this airport at this time of night, I'm gonna look like I know where I'm going and that I am certain about my surroundings." I picked up my bags and I went the rest of the way up the stairs to the eerily deserted landing.

"Walk as if you know where you're going." A Sheraton concierge approached offering me a room for 150 euro. I desperately needed a room with a bathtub. Accepting his suggestion I went in and negotiated for a room. With the relief of securing lodging, the day's trauma emerged. Tears began to roll down my face as the vivid image of the accident flooded my senses. Feeling the promise of safety in a comfortable room allowed me to share with the clerk the horrible accident I'd witnessed six hours earlier. He was very kind and got me a wonderful room with a bathtub that I soaked in until 2 a.m.

I did not go into hysterics or over-dramatize the situation or fall apart. I was blessed with my Sovereign Queen's guidance, demeanor, and grace. By calling on my benevolent Queen and the energy of the Lady of Compassion, I was able to be certain in my asking for lodging. I was able to stay reasonably calm in the face of chaos, and I was able to get what I needed the most; I was able to be purposely and conveniently at the airport to board my plane home the next morning.

I also had an absolutely wonderful and priceless gift waiting for me in the form of a business-class ticket, which meant a delicious meal and a lounge. I was able to sleep comfortably over the next 14 or 20 hours. I did indeed feel like the Sovereign Queen being cared for in the safety and comfort of the plane. I was headed home.

Once again the benevolent Queen in me and the mother bear took steps forward to make things right. This benevolent Queen lives deep inside of me. She is sovereign unto herself. She has the ability to shore up the walls, tighten up her resources, and take a good look at the pattern being repeated. She speaks out when it's time to take a new street instead of going down the same old path of problems.

When the martyr is in charge, a powerless weakness overcomes me and my whole being goes into victimhood again. NO is the answer: No, I am not a victim, I am determined, certain, and strong with a firm foundation under my feet. This is my Earth Mother. She reminds me who I am.

There are many circumstances in life that call upon us to engage our Sovereign Queen archetype and resolve situations quickly without drama. All women have access to this tool once we discover the many faces of the goddess at our fingertips. By understanding the Divine Feminine archetypes, I've learned so much more about who I am and who I am becoming as an empowered woman.

When you're in need of her, or suspect you are in need, here are some helpful questions to ask yourself:

What is my intention?
What am I responsible for?
What am I willing to compromise on?
What is my bottom line that I will not change?

When the answers to these questions become clear, we no longer linger in the space of not knowing. Our deeper knowing and truth enables us to stop the B.S. and take a committed stand for what we believe in. That is the moment we practice sovereignty. It is this strength of sovereignty that awakens the Benevolent Queen.

Special Gift

The process I used the night of the airport is a **Stress buster/ Energy Realignment.** I have a beautiful **Sovereign Queen meditation** for you to enjoy as well. You may get a copy for yourself by emailing me at **maryaine@return2joy.com.**

Please type "Evolutionary feminine" in the subject line and I will happily send both to you via your email address.

MaryAiñe Curtis, *Alchemist Author,* grew up during the tumultuous times of the 1950s and '60s in a family of six brothers and two younger sisters in a small, coastal town in California. Her life experience gave her the sacred contracts, experiences, trauma, and abuse that led to deep depression as well as domestic abuse as a young mother. Kept small by shame and guilt, for too long she accepted abuse as if she deserved it.

MaryAiñe describes herself as a misfit-spiritual-warrior-queen-rebel-starseed with an idealistic belief in the goodness of man and a hunger for world peace. Since 1996, she has offered women quantum leaps in healing to assist in the deep personal change that affects their entire lineage, uncovering and clearing unseen feelings that may be blocking the path to success. As a Holistic Therapist, Visionary and Personal Lifestyle Guide~ess, she offers the gifts of holistic healing arts, spiritual guidance, soul and transformation coaching, Reiki, and massage therapy—all built upon the miracle of loving herself as a whole, healed, and cherished daughter of Mother-Father God.

In her future memoir releasing in 2021, MaryAiñe shares her story of survival; and later, how life-changing pilgrimages to Ireland and France activated collective soul memories.

> *"I live a blessed life because I took the risk of looking deeply at my life patterns."*

Learn more at **maryainecurtis.com.**

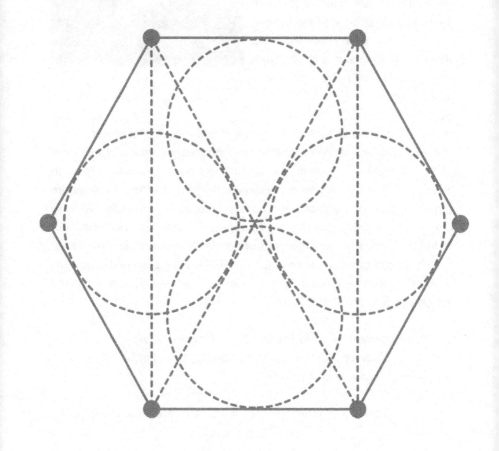

Sacred Union—
The Gift of Our Inner Marriage

BY COCO OYA CIENNAREY

Deep within the feminine psyche lives a longing, an urge to reconnect with the truth of who we are. We long to fully hear the call of the soul. Yet, we are often afraid to feel all the way within the self. We become afraid to inhabit our internal solitude. We condemn ourselves, say we are too needy, and renounce our wants and desires. We become lonely within ourselves, forget who we are, and forget we are divine beings worthy of receiving. The noise of the world takes over, and we let go of what makes our hearts sing. We shut down and become shadows of ourselves. I was there a little over a year ago, a lost soul in the wilderness of my life, willing myself to die.

I had been carrying the codes to unchain my sovereignty since I was a little girl, each forced intimate act and unwanted sexual encounter a blueprint to unlocking the riches of my heart. Yet I had no understanding that it was the drama and pain of this that would offer up the reward of reclaiming my Queendom. Everything I witnessed as a child was an unnatural way to love; I was caught up in false dogma, conditions, and game playing that caused untold traumas. It would take a lifetime to break the shackles of the past that conditioned me to follow down the same path of destructive relationships as my parents. I carried the shame in my body created by abuse. I was trained to be the good girl but told I was the bad girl. Either way it meant I had to disown and disconnect from the source of who I really was.

I would love to say that my first step of reclamation, leaving home at fifteen, was a great act of bravery. It wasn't; it was done out of pure survival. This act, my first do-or-die moment was a crossroads in which the voice of my soul stepped in and compelled me to stand in my truth. I was no longer willing to partake in or bear witness to the chaotic violence of home. This was the start of many moments that mysteriously and eventually led me to the path of living my best life and stepping into the new reality of living my dreams. Thirty-four years later, after that first soul stirring, I reached another crisis point, another do-or-die moment, that literally took me to the brink of death. Life had become so unbearable, the pain in my heart so heavy, the voices in my head so loud that I felt there was no way forward, backwards, or even sideward. I become hemmed in by my own maddening thoughts and failing body, and the choice whether to live or die felt almost taken out of my own hands.

Like novelist Paulo Coelho's character Veronika in *Veronika Decides to Die*, I wanted to die. I didn't want to have to face another day, I was tired of feeling lost. I was done with life. I was going home to meet my maker, to have it out with her. I wanted to know why my life had been so challenging. Why had I experienced so much trauma as a child? This wasn't the life that I knew I had come here to live. Little did I know at the time that the urge to die was, in fact, a call from my soul to leave behind the outdated version of myself and to step into my greatness. This was a wakeup call of epic proportions to rise from the ashes of my life and become a shining light for other women to see their own brilliance reflected back.

The morning of my near death, as the sun gleamed through the window crack signaling the dawning of another day, I willed my body to die. Laying there feeling the life drain out of me, I heard the constant buzzing of the phone. I was out of my body, and I couldn't respond. Message after message came in from loved ones who sensed something was wrong, a set of surreal divinely orchestrated events that brought five people's lives together into one singular convergence. I, locked inside my own mind, was sinking further into a black hole. Unable to respond with words, my body was shutting down, yet the people who loved me heard my virtual call and caught me just as I hit the bottom. I believe that day was guided by higher forces. Circumstances weaved together by the universe to create the perfect storm. Death kissed me on the lips that day, and the Great Mother brought me back to life.

I had a mission to fulfill, one that had been rumbling for many years previously, one that I had learned to drown out and ignore. It was the voice of my soul indicating the abundance of dreams awaiting me from the cosmos. I didn't believe I could have them; such was my lack of belief in life. Yet that morning changed all that. There was no mistaking divine assistance as help arrived at my door instigated by my friend sensing my soul from more than five thousand miles away. Her actions set into motion a chain of events that finally led to the police knocking down my door and saving my life. Much of that day I don't remember. What I do remember is, in the still of the night, as I was brought back home from the hospital, as I prayed to God and said I want to live, the most loving energy descended upon me. It encapsulated me in a warm marshmallow pink blanket of love, a love the likes of which I had never felt before, a love that began to remove the feelings of death from my bones as the false version of me began to fall away and my soul broke through.

This was a metaphorical death that needed to take place, the suicidal impulses too strong to ignore. I was being taken into the Void of the Divine Mother, being asked to leave my body, if only for a split second, so that my soul could fully jump in, as Death gently kissed me on the lips. So many of us hear this call to rebirth, but when this message is taken literally, sadly many take their own lives. I knew this was something more, my heart in crisis longing to surrender to the *internal* death and rebirth cycle. A transformation that can be painful as we learn to trust the wisdom of the body and learn to shift our narrative from suffering to surrender, from servant to sovereign, from death to rebirth, from suicide to soul awakening.

The journey is full of challenges as we shed our skins and become tender and raw. Like snakes, we go blind for a time until our new skin hardens and our eyes adjust to the new light. We go through a period of being in the unknown, feeling unsettled as we learn to have trust and faith in the process of metamorphosis. When we begin to shift into our greatness, when we finally surrender to who we are meant to be, there is often a lag in time. It is a time when we have no idea what is going on as the soul reunites and descends into the body. We are in the in-between space, the bridge between spirit and our human selves, the emptiness that comes from relinquishing the old and stepping into the new.

Often this feels like nothing is happening or that life has stopped moving, and you may find yourself imagining that "She" has abandoned you again. This is what it is like being in the womb of the Great Mother—the stillness, the dark of the void. This is a time that calls for presence, patience, and faith.

Know that this is no mistake; it is a necessary part of learning to trust the flow. We have to believe that even when the path ahead is dimly lit and we can only see one step ahead, the cosmos is guiding us all the way.

Nothing can grow without fallow times; we need to go within to grow into our becoming.

My father was a thief; he entered sacred places and took what was never his to take. He stole my essence and locked it away in a cage made of fear. I was forty-nine years old when I finally found the key to taking back what was held hostage from me for all those years. Victimhood made me unable to feel real love. I unconsciously harbored a repulsion of the masculine, so much so that I sabotaged all my relationships with men. I had a deep war raging inside between my inner masculine and inner feminine, whose love had been shattered from that first inappropriate touch that made me feel worthless and told me that I would have a thousand and one wounds to heal in the years to come. That touch made me leave my body and fragmented my soul so that it splintered away. I was unable to feel where my skin ended and another's began—boundaries ceased to be. I lost all sense of who I was, and my liberty was removed.

My sense of freedom was skewed; I learned from my father that to be free meant you do what you want and take what you want and hurt whoever is in your way to get your needs met. This, the distorted masculine, was the model I knew and I wanted nothing of. Yet, I attracted that pattern over and over, like bees to honey. I had been harboring a hidden pattern regarding men. Unconsciously, I submitted my will to theirs, a pattern hangover from my childhood. Unwittingly, I absorbed my mother's values of sacrifice as service. This dynamic is often so overlooked by women, the influence of the distorted masculine upon or own inner union, yet it was the missing piece of my death and rebirth. It would be the only way to know true freedom and finally bring my inner masculine and feminine into sacred union. I could now finally reclaim my Sovereignty and be the ultimate judge of myself. I was the *only* one who could ultimately say whether or not something was right for me.

I was taught to accommodate poor behavior, override my feelings, and ignore the redflags. I learned to ignore the inner wisdom and voice of my womb. All this resulted in my inner masculine having no need to listen to the inner feminine or to put her visions into action; he ruled the roost. He was noncommittal and lacked the ability to listen. For so long, my masculine devalued my feminine. My body had become a battleground. It was time to make it my inner feminine my ally, to drop in and listen to its deeper wisdom, to get real still and create room for the Divine aspect of the masculine to take up space, the same way I had to surrender and allow space for the universal forces to step in. I had to go in and find a way to clear the patterns and forgive myself.

I know deep in my heart that my inner masculine never wanted to harm me; it was all he had ever known. We struck up a dialogue. I asked him, "What is so lacking in the men that they need to feed off the life force of another just to feel alive?"

His response: "Men don't mean to be predators or be in lack; it is learned behavior. Their egos are told from a young age to be dominant, to be competitive, and to look out for number one. They are taught it's a dog eat dog world."

I knew it was true. We only have to look at our male leaders to see just how much this is playing out in the collective.

My inner masculine was tired of the old games and wanted to know the peace that comes from forgiveness. No longer at battle, we are in communication.

Forgiveness doesn't mean that you like what has been done; it's an awakening of acceptance that creates more space for healing in mind and body. Like reclaiming our sovereignty, forgiveness is a process, and it shouldn't be rushed. It takes time to move through its many layers and complexities. We learn to become more patient, compassionate, and accepting of all parts of the self and, in doing so, we are able to forgive others. We learn to hold our power one step at a time as we become the Queens of our Queendom. We explore and excavate both the dark and the light of our shadow, the parts we deem unworthy and those parts we lack confidence in claiming, all our gifts and all our gaffs. We are women learning to be gentle with ourselves.

We are beginning to wake up to the ancestral baggage handed down to us and placed over our original blueprint. We are beginning to see that within those patterns there are also gifts of gold, gifts that are byproducts of alchemizing our shadows. To transform the shadow is to experience pleasure and to anchor down heaven and earth. As we begin to dissolve the shadows that have kept us stuck, we stop asking for permission to *be* ourselves and we *save* ourselves. We hold within us the same Divine feminine spark as the Great Mother of all creation. She is we, and we are She.

She commands The Great Void, The Cosmic Womb, and just as a woman's body births life, so does the Cosmic Mother. She rebirths us if we allow her to. She held me tight through this Rite of passage and loved me back to life when I could not. She contains both masculine and feminine; her divine essence is the container that holds us all and is the support system that sustains life on earth. She is our base and our home. Our lives are a constant conversation with her great mystery if we choose to listen. During this reclamation, She spoke to me through my dreams, two of which were spontaneous shamanic waking dreams or visions in which I met and faced my father: once in the underworld to reclaim my two-year-old self, and once in the upper world, where I witnessed the karma between us dissolving to become no more. We stood together by the shores of the Great Void with total acceptance of the paths we had chosen to travel.

As I shift into a new era of sacred union within, I decree to always create a daily dialogue between my inner masculine and feminine as they calm each other's fears and doubts that sometimes arise when change is afoot. This is a new romance, and they are holding each other in a committed relationship, devoted to the cause of deeper connection and intimacy as they unite in service to the greater good. What my masculine needed was a cause, something to get his teeth into, to feel he was making a worthy contribution to life. I have become an observer to myself and a witness for them to have space to grow into. What possibilities could unfold as I allowed them to love and support one another? This was something I never knew before; I am now rewriting the script of what is possible in the name of love.

I have created ways in which each part of my masculine and feminine energies feels valued, regenerating all the energy previously used in conflict to create a new life. Where previously he dominated the feminine wrong to get his needs met, he now sees how much more the feminine can lead and give when he is loving and supportive. When he creates a safe container for her to flourish and flow, life affords them miracles every day. While he is the structure and form-maker, she is the visionary of the new ways; as they relax into one another, life pours through my body from its abundant ever-flowing springs. When we reach for the realms of sacred internal marriage, all that is in the way will rise as the masculine and feminine do their shadow dance. They tend to each other's wounds, holding them in compassionate love, so that we may receive the hidden potential that lies within.

I no longer settle for less than I want or desire. We each have a connection to source, to this great well of existence that wishes to shower us with love, abundance, and joy—and to fulfill our every wish beyond our wildness dreams. Life's impulse is to catapult us into the realm of infinite possibilities to create imaginings that benefit the good of the whole. This way of being, based on Tantric principles, has become a fundamental part of my existence. These principles have always been something previously known to me yet never fully lived. I am now being asked by the Great Mother to dive deeper into them; to embody them and make them my own; to emanate them at a core cellular level; to become a living prayer. When we truly embody our life experiences, life becomes so much easier to do.

For years I carried a belief that you had to do this life journey alone. I struggled, not wanting to live unable to receive help. Now I am open to the loving support of the universe, and I know I have a life worth living. To be sovereign means knowing my inner truth and being solid in who I am so that nothing can sway me off my path. Nothing can distract my focus from what I know I am here to be. No one can defer me from my calling, not even myself, because I have a passion for life pumping through my veins.

Our universal lack of Sovereignty is a crisis of desire, a desire to own our longing to know our true selves. To get comfortable with our longing, we need to develop the force within and make it strong enough so that we choose all of life—the good, the bad, and the ugly—and own it all. We need to embrace the gift of our wanting and feel worthy enough to receive. We would not have individual desires at all if all we were here to do was exist.

As we grow into our Sovereignty, we learn to ride the waves of emotions. When we open to life, we become supported. Life meets us as we step onto the next level of purpose. When we open to life, it can literally change over-night; I am testimony to that. Life shifts us into a space-time reality where doors open, gifts appear, and opportunities land on our doorstep as we get into alignment with the truth of who we are.

Special Gift

**FEMININE FUNDAMENTALS—
8 PILLARS TO UNEARTHING THE TRUE YOU**

This 15 page PDF introduces the '8 Pillars'—the guiding principles of the 'Feminine Fundamentals' way. The guide also outlines how working with the 'Elements of Nature' provides the bedrock upon which the Pillars stand. It offers tips, tools and practices on connecting to the voice of your heart and igniting your desires.

Access here: **https://creativelycoco.com/gift**

Coco Oya CiennaRey is a UK-based creative, poet, soul guide, and writer published in several anthologies. Her creativity is informed by her journey as a devotee of the Tantric path (an embodied path of self-liberation) and her experience within the field of trauma. She has always felt a call to channel the Voice of the Divine Feminine. Often thought-provoking, always heartfelt, her work speaks of the

sacred wisdom stored in the body, the nonlinear nature of trauma and the embodiment of soul. In recognition of the human capacity to take the pains and chaos of life and transmute them into purpose, passion, and beauty, she believes that our innate connection to the natural world can heal humanity.

Deeply sensitive and highly empathic, through guidance from the seen and unseen world, Coco's passion is to share her journey to inspire and assist those that are ready to reclaim their authentic voice. Her gift as an intuitive and collective collaborator affords her the ability to understand the root of a given situation and bring core issues to light for release and healing. Her growing movement and community called Feminine Fundamentals speak to the current worldwide evolutionary shift as we collectively balance the masculine and feminine principles within and without for both men and women. Feminine Fundamentals explores the concepts of relationships, intimacy, and connection as spiritual practices and aims to gather like-minded souls who are ready to embrace their soul gifts. We thrive through community and in doing so we re-establish the connection to ourselves, to one another, to nature, and to Source; all of which are the fundamental building blocks of life.

Learn more at **https://creativelycoco.com/**

#WriteratHeart #CreativebyNature #LoverforLife #SirenofSoul

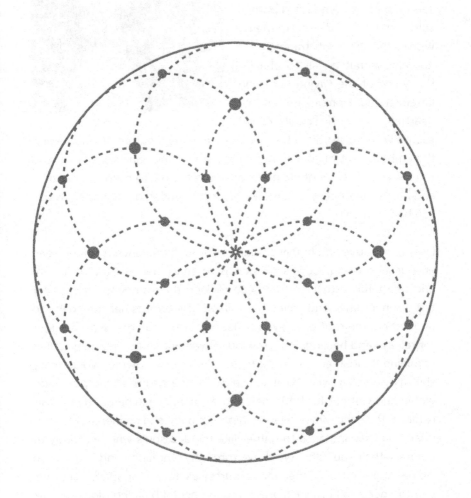

Arm From Heaven

BY WINDY COOK

·······⟨⟩·······

Our lady of the rose crown,
know that the biggest gift you will receive right
now is found within you,
you hold the key.
The biggest gift is your open heart;
your shifted perspective.
Your understanding of the bigger picture.
Your biggest gift is who you are and all you
stand for.
Your power. Your beauty.
Your strength and courage in the face of
adversity.
Your love...
and your pure light.
That is the gift. Find the gift
and use it to help others.
Use it to heal.
To grow, to expand and to awaken.
There is no time to waste.
Heal and be healed.
Be the Truth. Be the Way. Be the Light.

— *ALANA FAIRCHILD,* "MOTHER MARY ORACLE
CARD DECK"

What is your greatest fear? What makes you tremble and shake? For me, it's
drowning. Drowning in deep water and I cannot resurface to take a breath.
Coming in at a close second is standing up in front of a group of people and
talking. Interestingly, it's not *all* people, it's adults and primarily adult men.
The very thought of standing up in front of a crowd of people looking at me
makes my palms sweat and my heart pound.

When I was teaching elementary school, I relished watching my bright-eyed students listen to my daily lesson. I loved answering their questions, listening to their ideas and exploring unknowns together. Never nervous, I felt comfortable and in my element. Children are authentically personable with their quirky selves, and perfection isn't required.

When I became a mother of twins, teaching third grade was no longer my calling—although teaching still was. Teaching has been my passion since as far back as I can remember. It is what I'm here to do. Nothing gives me more joy than helping people learn so that they can grow, expand, and awaken.

One of my favorite teaching experiences was my internship in undergraduate school in which I taught cognitive restructuring in an outpatient setting at the local hospital. Teaching patients struggling with depression and mental health issues—the correlation between thoughts, feelings, and behavior—brought me joy.

This spring, I finally had the courage to teach my first ThetaHealing® class. ThetaHealing is a mediation technique that utilizes a spiritual philosophy for improvement of mind, body, and spirit. ThetaHealing is similar to cognitive restructuring in the sense that it enables one to access and clear negative thoughts so that positive changes can be made to one's life.

I'd been a successful elementary teacher for years, so I was stumped. Why did teaching my first ThetaHealing class take courage? What was I so afraid of?

It took courage because, for the first time in my life, I was teaching adults.

·······෴·······

The clock is ticking in the crowded room of the City Hall. People are packed together like sardines waiting for the opportunity to speak. It's a new ordinance my neighbors are here for; an ordinance that prohibits one from walking out their gate to open space. I'm here with my husband because we use our back gate on a daily basis to walk outside on the mesa. In fact, the open space is the main reason why we purchased our home.

Being under the wide open sky is where I feel alive. There are miles of beautiful trails stretching through the tall grass, evergreen trees, and red rocks. Now, after 20 years, the city is worried about the environmental impact that people are having on the open space and the city is putting their foot down with a hefty fine of $2,600 if you choose to break the ordinance.

I know what I have to do. I have to get up to the podium when my name is called and talk in front of a big group of people. I not only have to talk, but I have to be articulate, intelligent, well informed, and *convincing*. Convincing a group of men that the new ordinance should be rescinded. I look around the room, and my heart begins to pound. My hands become sweaty, and there is no place to run. I feel like I am having a panic attack and I'm suddenly ashamed about it. Why aren't other people nervous?

Several months ago, there I sat in a sacred circle with a priestess during a 13 Moon Mystery School gathering developed by Ariel Spilsbury, exploring the primal goddess, one of the archetypes of the divine feminine. For years, I had been searching for answers to my lack of empowerment.

Where was my sovereignty?

> "For the last millennia, virtually everything we've come to think of as spiritual practice has been designed by and for masculine consciousness and masculine bodies. Truly feminine forms of worship, awakening, and transformation were marginalized at best and often violently persecuted."
>
> —ARIEL SPILSBURY, "FEMININE ALCHEMY"

Violently persecuted.

Oh, how I somehow, somewhere, remember that.

"What is holding you back?" The priestess asks. I hear her question echo inside my brain.

"What is holding you back from accessing your raw, primal power that is your birthright?" she asks.

I shudder and a voice deep in my solar plexus answers, "I'm afraid I will be misunderstood."

"Misunderstood?" she answers back.

"I'm afraid that if I allow my primal, wild self to emerge, it'll be too much."

"Too much?"

"If I am wild, primal and free I will be perceived as strange, not sweet or nice."

"What is wrong with that?"

"If you're not sweet but wild and powerful, you are misunderstood, alienated, and rejected by your loved ones and community."

"It's not safe to be that powerful." My tears of sorrow begin to swell.

"Why?"

I feel my nose dripping.

The priestess notices.

"Your nose, dear one."

I reach for a tissue and wipe blood. The blood is there to remind me.

Remind me of what?

I step into the hot bath and watch the water envelop my navel. It feels good to be in the tub. I close my eyes and allow my breath to take me to the place of quiet solitude—a place where I can search for the answers that I seek.

Why is my nose bleeding? I ask myself.

A vision appears, and it's from a time long ago.

It's centuries ago, and I'm in a European cottage with dried herbs hanging and a kettle on a fire. A group of men enter through the carved wooden door. There's a struggle and I'm carried out. Where are they taking me? I try to break free but am quickly roped. What have I done? An iron ball is wrapped to my foot. My arms and legs are roped as I'm dropped into the dark water. Screams fill my lungs and I try to set myself free. The weight of the iron takes me down to an unknown, terrifying place, and my screams are silenced with gulps of water. I look up hoping to see a merciful arm to grasp, only to sink deeper.

I cannot resurface. Was I imagining this or recalling a past life?

Was it my past life or was it an ancestor's life on my maternal line? Questions swirled around like ripples of bath water. Was I tapping into what psychiatrist Carl Jung described as the "collective unconscious"?

Could I liberate myself from my fears by remembering the trauma of what so many women had experienced in the past?

Was it my terrifying past?

> "Real liberation comes not from glossing over
> or repressing painful states of feeling, but only
> from experiencing them to the full."
>
> —*CARL JUNG*

Wikipedia states, "Beginning in the 1400s, widespread beliefs in superstition, lack of education, illiteracy, caste system, male dominance and economic dependency of women on men contributed to the belief that certain women were witches. Although it is not possible to ascertain the exact number, modern scholars estimate around 40,000 to 50,000 women, particularly from the 15th-18th centuries, were convicted of witchcraft. Common methods of execution were hanging, drowning, and burning."

Was my lack of sovereignty a result of trauma and possibly murder? I certainly love herbs and the healing arts, but I've never been into black magic, cauldrons, or putting curses on people. On Halloween each year I've never even wanted to dress up like a witch or anything scary, for that matter. I've dressed up as a gypsy, angel, fairy, goddess, and a butterfly. Never a witch.

The reality of what I needed to do was setting in. Finding my power and my precious sovereignty meant diving into my unconscious, or "shadow." I needed to look into the personal qualities that I was repressing, ignoring, and denying. (Learning-mind.com)

I knew a place where I could go, a place where I could find some answers to the questions I was seeking: the International ThetaHealing Institute in Montana.

Have you ever been to Montana? The sky goes on forever and the mountains rise to eternity. Everything is big in Montana. The trees are big, the rocks are big. The answers I seek are big. I guess that's why they call it "Big Sky" country. For five years now, I've been traveling to Montana to take ThetaHealing classes.

I have taken several years of practitioner and instructor courses to explore my subconscious, reprogram my mind to awaken my potential, and to evolve. For years, I'd been certified to teach the Basic ThetaHealing class, and yet something stood in my way. I was paralyzed fear.

This past summer, I was taking an Instructor course and doing a hands-on exercise with another ThetaHealer. We were exploring the obstacles that were possibly preventing us from successful careers. We were doing a "digging" exercise in which each person asks questions in a relaxed or "Theta state" with muscle testing. Muscle testing is a helpful technique for exploring subconscious beliefs and thoughts that are often buried either in a person's childhood, in a person's DNA from ancestors, or in a person's karmic or past life.

My ThetaHealing partner asks me to close my eyes, take a deep breath, and relax. Then she asks me, "Why aren't you teaching?"

"I don't know."

"What if you did know?"

My mind scans back to a forgotten time. To a time before even I can recognize. A vision comes into focus:

I'm standing in a beautiful, ancient forest. Animals surround me and I'm walking amongst them. I can speak the language of the trees and the stars. I wear a velvet cloak of emerald green, and a crown of roses adorn my head. I am a sovereign goddess. I have the wisdom of the ancient stones and knowledge of the heavens.

I am in that place of my higher self. The details of what, how, or why do not matter. It just IS.

"What are you doing in your vision?" asks my ThetaHealing partner.

"I'm sharing my wisdom and guiding people," I say. "Teaching people."

"Are they listening?"

"Some are... but... "

"But what?"

"Men are laughing at me and ridiculing me. They throw stones at me and tell me that I'm crazy and that I should be punished. They come after me and... "

I muscle test "yes" that I hold the beliefs of, "If I am a healer I will be killed," and "If I step into my power as a teacher, I will be disrespected and laughed at."

"I am not safe to be my sovereign self," I say.

"These seem to be old, outdated beliefs in your subconscious that quite possibly have been holding you back," my partner says. "Do I have your permission for the Divine or Creator to send you unconditional love to heal you from the shock and trauma you experienced during this time?"

"Yes," I whisper

My eyes are closed and my breathing slows down. I'm filled with a beautiful peaceful sense of peace and love.

Resolution.

Several minutes pass and then my partner asks me a question.

"What did you learn from being disrespected, laughed at, and ridiculed?"

I think back to that moment and my mind spans space and time. Finally an answer comes into my heart.

"I learned humility and compassion."

Then my partner asks if I'd like to clear and resolve my beliefs around teaching adults, especially men, so that I can teach cognitive restructuring techniques and ThetaHealing courses.

"Yes!"

Then comes the beautiful golden nugget of ThetaHealing, witnessing the energetic shift of clearing the beliefs that no longer serve one's highest good and replacing these old thoughts with vibrationally higher, more positive, and more intelligent ones.

"Would you like to know what it feels like to understand humility and compassion free from punishment and persecution *and* what it feels like to walk in your *sovereignty*?" my partner asks.

"Yes!"

"Would you like some new beautiful affirmations and downloads?" my ThetaHealing partner asks with a smile.

"Yes."

Downloads are new thoughts and affirmations that are integrated with a request to the Divine or Creator—also known as the "Energy of All That Is."

My ThetaHealing partner prays, "Creator of All that Is, it is requested to download Windy with the Divine's perspective of what it feels like to be confident, self-assured, and empowered, with the Divine's perspective of what it feels like to walk with *sovereignty*."

"Yes!" I answer and the most beautiful peaceful feeling fills my body. My eyes are closed and I take a deep, cleansing breath.

Breathing out, I notice an energetic shift, a shift of consciousness. My entire being feels lighter. A deep awareness sets in my heart-space.

Resolution.

I've finally identified the reason for my fear of speaking in front of people, especially men.

·······⎯⎯∙⎯⎯·······

"Windy Cook?" I hear my name being called, and the panel of City Council members turn to look in my direction. "Yes," I reply, and walk slowly to the podium. It's my turn to speak. I'm shaking and take a deep breath. For a moment, I am suddenly aware that I'm about to face one of my greatest fears. I may be laughed at and ridiculed. I may stutter and embarrass myself. But a primal instinct comes over me. I root down and find my ankles on the earth, and I speak from my heart.

"Good evening City Council," I say. "I am here with my husband tonight to speak against the ordinance that prohibits one from using their gate to access open space."

I feel vulnerable, I'm *all in*, and yes, I'm in the arena, as Brene' Brown would say.

I take another deep breath, anchoring my words from a place of *love*. Love toward the land and love toward my relationship with Mother Earth, nature and all her creatures. "We'd like to collaborate with the city," I say. We hope to plant the native grass seeds of the mesa, step lightly and avoid using the same path from our gate. Preservation is our goal, too."

I notice the mayor of the town begin to smile. After several more state-ments, I conclude with "thank you"—and my husband and I walk outside and leave City Hall. As we turn to go, I feel a man gently touch my arm.

"Good job," my neighbor says to me as we leave. I smile back and quietly laugh to myself.

It's the morning of the Basic ThetaHealing class and I'm preparing to teach the class for the first time. I'm nervous but excited for this day to finally arrive. The Basic ThetaHealing class is the first class that introduces the ThetaHealing technique. It's the foundation for all to follow, and it's life-changing. I step outside into the morning air. My eyes look to the sky, and it's a beautiful sunrise.

The sky is filled with promise, puffy clouds, and pink streams of light. Out of the north, a narrow cloud pierces through the horizon. The cloud looks like something. It's quite large and it begins to take human shape. I stand with an upward glance and I gasp. The cloud forms a long extended arm. At the end of the arm is a hand. The hand is pointing to my house.

It's an arm from heaven.

Windy Cook is the best-selling author of *The Sisterhood of The Mindful Goddess* and contributing author to three books in the best-selling *New Feminine Evolutionary* series: *New Feminine Evolutionary, Sacred Body Wisdom, and Set Sail.* She is also the author of "Following Windy", an interactive blog for hopeful mothers struggling with fertility issues at "Moms Like Me". Windy is a graduate of the Journey  of Young Women Mentoring Girls Certificate Training and enjoys holding "Winds of Change" sacred circles for girls, mothers, and women of all ages. She also has formal training as a physio-neuro trainer, is certified in Reiki II, and is a ThetaHealing™ practitioner and instructor.

Windy's path includes work as a family therapist at Denver Children's Home for troubled youth and as a third-grade teacher in an inner-city public school for gifted and talented children. She holds a master's degree of Social Work from the University of Denver as well as a master's degree in Educational Psychology from the University of Colorado, Denver. She is Phi Beta Kappa from Colorado State University.

Passionate about philanthropic causes, Windy supports educational, environmental, and other nonprofit programs that promote the well-being of women and children. Windy can be found in a nearby yoga studio, hiking, playing with her children, picking sage, walking her dog, or riding her bike in open space. She lives in Colorado with her beloved husband, three children, and golden retriever.

Learn more at **www.windycook.com.**

Special Gift

FREE 30-MIN THETAHEALING
INTRODUCTORY SESSION

Type the words "ThetaHealing Intro Session" into the subject line and I'll reach out to schedule your session!

Access here: **www.windycook.com/connect**

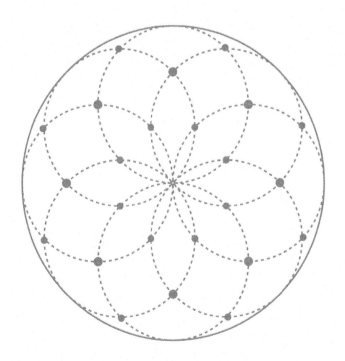

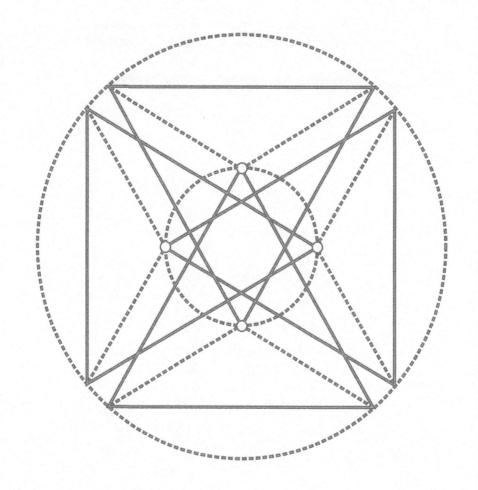

Waking Up Sleeping Beauty

BY AURORA FARBER

My life has often felt like a fairy-tale; even my name has shaped the script of my own gilded story book. "Aurora" means the dawn and is the name of a fairy-tale princess destined to fall asleep at the dawn of her feminine power.

Like Sleeping Beauty, my power has been nestled in deep slumber for much of my life. My ideas of femininity and purpose were modeled after the princesses of my childhood, and these role models shaped my perception with a script of rules on how to behave. With a sharp spindle, the teachings of shadowy patriarchal power pricked the minds of thousands of little girls like me, casting a veil over our sovereignty as we succumbed to the belief that our value was tied to beauty and wit, and that our awakening would come in the form of a handsome prince.

Instead of a fateful kiss, my sovereign awakening has come to me in bits and pieces, like a patchwork quilt, sewn together from the mystery and magic of synchronicity, music, visions and dreams... These gifts from the fairies that wake me up again and again, as I lose myself in the familiar scaffolding of my princess dreams. These gifts from the Divine have blessed me with an inner knowing that I am held, even cradled in a warm blanket of magic moments that hold my divine humanity with tender care.

Come with me as I unravel and reweave my story of sovereign awakening. May it inspire you to look at your own mythic story and awaken the sleeping beauty within.

MALEFICENT POWER

I'm walking down a street filled with shops and I see the weather
changing. But it's not just a storm that's coming... it is Her. I
begin to run, because Her power is untamed. Wild. Fierce.
Destructive. Free. I run across the street, and just as She is about
to overcome me, I shout, "I am Her. This is my body."
I chant this over and over, and she pauses and does not suck
me into the wind. Suddenly a golden swing is let down from the
sky. I sit on it and, as it lifts me above the storm, I see the ocean
ahead. I'm afraid, but I think, "I just need to get to the ocean.
Then if I fall, the sea will catch me."

I spent much of my life afraid of my own power, afraid to follow my heart and inner guidance because I might be criticized for being too much or condemned for not being enough. I chose to stay small and silent with my passion and purpose tucked away, drifting in a restless sleep.

I had been taught that power was dangerous, capable of causing harm if not wielded properly. But what was proper? There were so few models of feminine power for me to follow. So like many women, I adopted masculine ways of striving, pursuing, working, and achieving to get ahead—regardless of the cost.

I did not want to be like Maleficent, the dark fairy who suffered from the wounds of sisterhood—jealousy, comparison and judgment—and cursed Sleeping Beauty with her christening gift of death. With Maleficent as a role model, I feared that claiming my power might result in annihilation of myself or others. So I contained myself and my dreams.

I needed something catalytic to wake me from my fear of being "too much or not enough." It was then that the Divine Feminine came to me in a dream as a gale force wind that threatened to destroy the structures that I had built my life upon.

Her energy was powerful, untamed; so connected to the earth and elements, so raw and fierce, yet loving. I longed to commune with Her, but I didn't know how. I was tired of running, so I stopped, and in that sacred pause I claimed Her and my body again and again.

"I am Her. This is my body."

This was the magical incantation that began my journey on the winding, spiral path of the Divine Feminine mysteries. In an act of grace, the golden swing showed me the way home—to myself, to the sea, and to the Divine Feminine in me. From that high aerial view, I saw the path forward and the first step to reclaim my power and soul essence: surrender.

Surrendering into Her arms was not easy. My soul voice knew that "If I fall, She will catch me," but I didn't fully trust this inner knowing. I had been taught to be in control, to see and plan ahead, but this had only resulted in constant vigilance that was exhausting.

I wanted to let this belief die, but death was also something I was taught to fear. Maleficent's curse of death had ruined Aurora's christening. Or had it? I began to see that perhaps the gift of death was the greatest gift of all, for in death there is the possibility of rebirth, like the last gift given to Aurora, the gift of awakening.

As I began to let old habits and patterns from my childhood scripts die, I discovered a whole new world of the Divine Feminine mysteries and the spiral path that would lead me to my sacred work as a Feminine Leadership Coach and Priestess. Transmuting the story of feminine power from "maleficent to magnificent" pointed me in the direction of my purpose, but to fully step onto the path, just like Sleeping Beauty, I needed a little help from the fairies.

FAIRY GODMOTHERS

Something is rising up in me. From my womb to my heart, I feel
a buzzing that gets caught in my throat. I'm choking, trying to hold
it back. Trying not to be so emotional, trying to be back in control.
My throat aches and tears stream down my face signaling my body's
refusal to put on that well-worn mask of perfection. And then she
takes off her gloves. She runs free, creating worlds with the magic in
her hands as she sings "Let it go."

For years, I believed that my mask of perfection would help me gain the love and validation I desired. Adorning myself in Sleeping Beauty's gifts of beauty, grace, and goodness, I sacrificed my own voice and opinion to be palatable to others. I relied on my well-worn mask of perfection until it was zapped by the magic presence of two women named Elsa.

The first time I watched the Disney film *Frozen* and saw Elsa take off her gloves and transform into a Sovereign Queen fully owning her magic, something awoke within. This new archetype of feminine power illuminated with crystal clarity the truth of my perfectionism. My mask was a frozen facade of who I thought I needed to be and, like an iceberg, my true power was frozen and unseen, even to me.

Like Elsa, I was afraid of my power. *"What if I hurt someone? What if I use my power in anger or greed? What if my power makes someone else feel powerless?"*

Seeing Elsa own her magic sparked new hope, and I began to ask different questions. *"What if my power is magical? What if I can create new worlds and new stories? What if my power can heal my own heart and even heal the world?"*

To claim this rising power, I knew I had to take off my own "gloves" and let go of my mask of perfection. *Let it go, let it go,* I sang—crying, cracking and straining my voice as I choked on the words *"that perfect girl is gone."* This song was an incantation that began a healing in me and challenged both my belief system and my vocal range.

I began vocal lessons with an amazing opera singer, also named Elsa. She was like my human fairy godmother: her lessons and presence helping me wake up my true power. My "perfect girl" showed up to every lesson. As I cringed with each crack of my voice, with every silent self-judgment of my voice not being strong or pretty enough, Elsa stood by me; guiding me, seeing my beauty and power anyway.

One day, Elsa's lesson left me shaking and in a torrent of tears. *I just can't do it "right"... I'll never be able to sing... I'll never be able to let it go.* Feeling hopeless and powerless, Elsa's words that day helped me remove my gloves and loosen the mask of perfection that kept my power contained.

As an opera singer, when you sing you must give it 100%.
Not 75 or even 99.9%... you must send your voice across a very
loud orchestra.
Stop trying to sound pretty. Just be authentic. Own your power.
I don't want to hear pretty Aurora.
I want to hear A-ROAR-a.

Elsa saw something beyond my mask of perfection; she saw the lion in me. When I got home, I belted that song in the shower during the weeks that followed. This daily ritual unleashed my fierce, feminine, feline power. I stood naked, raw, and liberated as my mask fell in pieces at my feet. My voice was finally free. My heart cracked open in gratitude for the Elsa's—my fairy godmothers who reminded me of my timeless magic—even when I had forgotten.

THE PRINCE WITHIN

I am at a party and I see a man with a wig.
I want to talk to him, but he dismisses me with a single glance.
Feeling rejected, I collapse into a wheelchair and wheel myself
out to a baseball field.
I see an obese woman and several other people
All singing and praising the Divine.
I'm drawn to the energy of this woman.
I'm magnetized to her Joy.

When I was a little girl, I hoped that like Sleeping Beauty, I would marry Prince Charming and live happily ever after. As I grew up I discovered other passions, but in my heart I believed that I would not be whole until a handsome prince and True Love's kiss completed me.

As synchronicity follows intention, that's exactly what happened and the romance with my prince unfolded like a fairy-tale. A chance meeting at a bar led to a two-week visit to the beautiful island of Taiwan where my prince lived. Nine months later, we were married and on our way to our honeymoon destination, Princeville, on the island of Kauai. Even our wedding ceremony was called, "Prince Pu and Princess Flutterbye's Search for Happily Ever After."

My prince and I went on many amazing travel adventures and after five years of marriage, we decided to embark on the greatest adventure of all and start our family. We had two amazing children and though I loved being a mom and wife, something was disrupting my "happily ever after". Inside I yearned for more and I felt guilty about it. After all, I had met and married a prince. I was the Queen of my Queendom. Why then, did I have this gnawing yearning to be more?

The answers came to me in a dream, showing me how I was afraid of my drive and desire; I was afraid of my own inner masculine, and I didn't trust that I could show up for myself. I was projecting my masculine power onto my husband, while pushing my own desire away, afraid that I'd become like "Mr. Wig", the character who embodied the energy of the toxic masculine. Disconnected from his heart and using power for personal gain, a single glance from "Mr. Wig" collapsed my desire, so I would seek sanctuary in the feminine, in my dream character "Joy". But this joy that magnetized me and healed me was also imbalanced—I was weighed down with over-giving and over-responsibility. Filling myself with the joy of motherhood, while stuffing down my other desires.

I began working with this dream so that I could come into balance. Using a writing process called active imagination, I scripted a conversation between the two characters. As each of them released judgment of the other, they saw unique gifts emerge. In an act of integration, they decided to tango; Mr. Wig took the lead and provided a solid frame that allowed Joy to dance the full expression of her desires.

I painted their tango to seal my commitment to my inner masculine and feminine: this sacred marriage of the noble, protective masculine that champions the feminine to fearlessly flow, her creative spark lighting up the darkness like the fiery, red gown painted across my canvas. This painting, called *Feminine Fire*, awakened my sovereign purpose—my soul purpose that had nothing to do with anyone or anything outside of me. Fortified by my own inner marriage, I discovered my life's work: to help other women ignite their Feminine Fire—the magic, mission, and magnificence that is sourced from within.

HAPPILY EVER AFTER

> *Elsa hears the call again, but this time she doesn't ignore it. She moves toward it, trusting it, even though its source is unknown. Her intuition tells her that this voice is benevolent. As she battles and befriends the sea and then steps onto Ahtohallan, I cry tears of remembrance. I know this place. I know this mother. I know this call. I've been hearing the call too, deep within the chambers of my heart. This call to "Show Yourself" sung by an artist named AURORA.*

I began 2020 as I always do now: in the mystery, surrendering to receive. I love this liminal time, that like the dawn, holds the promise of something exciting to come. I no longer make resolutions and set goals. January is my dreaming time—to go within and listen, and watch and wait for the seeds and signs that will guide me for the year.

One of those signs came to me as a call: the *Ah-ha, ah-ha's* sung by a voice of my own namesake. The message and music of *Frozen 2* arrived like a magical breadcrumb to guide me forward, especially this year when my heart is calling me to expand and serve on a deeper level.

Eight years ago, a gale force wind woke me up and led me into the unknown. This path of initiation hasn't been easy, but every day I'm grateful for the tools I have to wake up from my temptation to go back to sleep. Each day my prayer is like an incantation, "I am willing. Show me the way." This mantra helps me live more freely as I dance in the mystery of now.

Still there's a part of me that holds back; the part of me who like Elsa clings to the comfort of what is familiar; the part that doesn't believe that I can live in full expression of my divine purpose; the part that wonders, *"What if I really let my purpose guide me and it overwhelms me? What if like the lullaby 'All Is Found,' I dive too deep and then I drown?"*

The fairy-tales of my childhood taught me to settle for comfort, to count my blessings and strive for a fairy-tale ending. The path of my life was clear. To fulfill my divine purpose I only needed *to be rescued, to marry the prince, and live happily ever after.*

I can no longer ignore this call to create a new story of feminine sovereignty. This call and response between the Elsa and Aurora in me beckons me with a daring vision of feminine power—sovereign power that is connected to life and the elements, that bridges the world of the human and divine. This new archetype of the Priestess rising. She who can spin new worlds into being in the palm of her hands. She who is the missing fifth element that brings healing and integration to a world broken by patriarchal fear and greed.

As I see Elsa choose to dive deep into the unknown, I know I can trust my soul voice as it calls me to forward. I can "show myself" and walk in ecstasy upon this priestess path. I can embrace my mission and be a catalyst for its unfolding. I can finally truly surrender, "let it go," and trust the divine wisdom I received eight years ago, *"If I fall, the sea will catch me. She will catch me."*

A NEW DAWN

I see a spinning heart that turns into an erupting volcano.
The lava floats down, destroying the old, creating new pathways
As it hits the shore and forms new land.
In the distance I see myself and a fleet of women,
Each of us in our own boat, coming toward the island.
Holding our feminine fire at our heart-center
We sing songs of power, love and wisdom.
Above us, a dragon lights the sky with his fiery blaze...

On my fiftieth birthday, I received this vision of a fleet of sovereign women changing the world through fiery songs of the heart. Without knowing how to make this a reality, I continue to hold it in my heart, share it through writing and speaking online, and pass this light of hope to those willing to receive it.

The dragon's presence always puzzled me, until I was gifted with another sign that helped me understand, just as the pandemic of 2020 began...

Above us, a dragon lights the sky with his fiery blaze...
And a golden phoenix swoops down, responding to our song
with Her tearful cry.

I realize now that our heart songs are a call to the Divine Feminine, a call to awaken Her within each of us. This call is an echo of our own longing to be whole, to be alive and in communion with our Divine purpose. This sacred call pierces through the pain of patriarchal stories and structures, as healing phoenix tears create a rebirth of something unimaginably beautiful—a new Earth formed by the union of the Sacred Masculine and the Divine Feminine.

My journey has shown me that the Universe longs for and assists our great awakening. As old stories and structures die, there is something wonderful that awaits us in the new dawn. In that liminal light, the fairies celebrate our rebirth and shower us with gifts of magic and synchronicity to light the dark path ahead. With our awakened, sovereign hearts, we create new fairy-tales of limitless light and infinite love, tales that ignite hope in the new world for generations to come.

A SOVEREIGN AWAKENING

Once upon a time there lived a princess,
born both human and divine.
Made of clay and stardust, she came into the world
to unite that which was separate
and heal the world with the love blazing in her heart.

Her power was sourced from love and wisdom
and in the joy of communing with life.
The earth was her playground
and the fairies were her friends.

With her every step she honored the land
and the elements with reverence.
Blessed with everything needed to fulfill her divine mission,
a seed of sovereign awakening was planted
deep within her soul.

But for this seed to germinate,
she had to enter the darkness.
She had to forget her true self and go to sleep.

Embraced by the unknown, she became undone.
forgetting her power,
She gave it away or projected it on to others
and replaced her inner truth
with new rules on how to be "good" and "perfect"
to feel loved and valued.

Deaf to the whisperings of her soul voice,
she heard only voices outside herself...
Voices that condemned her as "not enough" or "too much,"
until she embodied the false reflections she received.

She had forgotten that she was both human and divine,
with the power to birth new worlds,
new life, and new stories into being.

Her sacred flame smoldered
underneath the scripts that others had written.
With her spirit consumed and her power drained,
she fell into a somber slumber
lasting for thousands of years until the great awakening came.
Then the seed finally sprouted and bloomed
with True Love's sovereign kiss.

In that moment, her eyes wide, her heart open,
her sacred flame once again ignited,
she rose up like a fiery phoenix.
Pulsating. Rising. Soaring.
Her power now sourced from the temple of her heart.

She released a piercing cry of truth and liberation.
All the stories of unworthiness incinerated in one breath,
as a song reclaiming her sacred, divine humanity
sent sparks of remembrance across the sky.

"I am she.
I am SHE."

She had lost herself in order to find herself,
and now that she had awakened her sovereign power
it would never be put to sleep again.

Aurora Anurca Farber, Feminine Leadership Coach, Spiritual Guide, Writer, Speaker and modern-day Priestess, is on a mission to help women step into leadership and ignite their "Feminine Fire"—the three flames of POWER, LOVE and WISDOM that are the key to awakening the new feminine evolutionary consciousness that will heal our world. She helps women burn away limiting beliefs, align with their  feminine moon rhythm, and embody their mythic purpose in the world.

Aurora holds honors degrees in Literature and Foreign Language, along with a professional certification in Coaching. She is a Priestess Initiate of The 13 Moon Mystery School, and as a Temple Guide Trainer of the Priestess Presence Temple, she mentors women in how to create sacred space and become Temple Guides in their communities. She is a co-author of 4 books in the The New Feminine Evolutionary series: *The New Feminine Evolutionary; Pioneering the Path to Prosperity; Sacred Body Wisdom* and *Sovereign Unto Herself.* She is also a featured writer and artist in *Voices of the Avalonian Priestesses.*

Through private coaching, online programs, women circles and retreats, Aurora creates "sacred spaces" for women to be held, witnessed and loved exactly as they are right here, right now. Her guiding vision is a world of women claiming their creative powers, loving their body temples, and being beacons of fierce wisdom as they burn away archaic, limiting beliefs and light the world on fire with love.

Learn more at **AuroraFarber.com.**

Special Gift

THE FEMININE LUNAR ARCHETYPE QUIZ

Awaken your intuition, align with your feminine rhythm and sync up to the magic of the moon with the Feminine Lunar Archetype Quiz.

Activate new feminine archetypes of Mother, Queen, Goddess and Sage that can help empower your own mythic tale of love, light, and magic.

Access here: **www.aurorafarber.com/quiz**

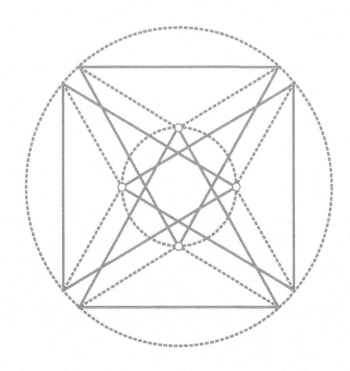

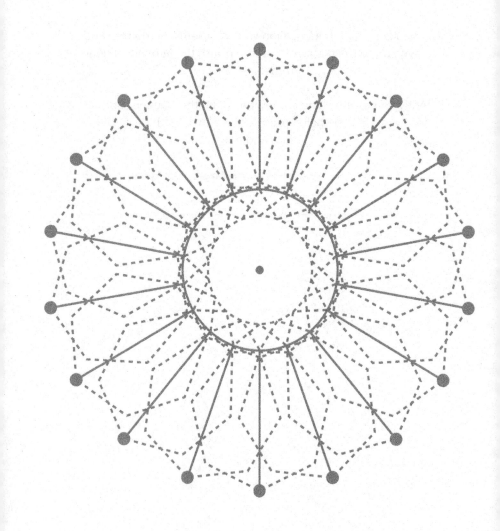

Divinely Aligned Sovereignty

BY DEBORAH HARLOW

I sat on the bench next to my dad, feeling the warmth of the sun on my cheeks, smelling the salt in the air from the spray of the ocean. We sat side by side, basking in the moment of our shared happy place. My dad opened the white paper bag and pulled out a donut for each of us. I raised the maple bar to my mouth and closed my eyes in pure delight.

As we sat in silence enjoying our treats, I could feel anxious questions bubbling inside me. After I had consumed enough of the donut to feel ready, I turned to my dad and asked, "Why did that lady talk to me like she knew me?"

He turned to me and smiled a small grin. He placed his cup of tea on the bench and replied, "Deborah, my little copper knob, you are an old soul. You won't fully understand that now but don't worry. I'll always be by your side looking out for you."

As we walked into the house later that afternoon, mom asked where we had been, without really needing an answer, since her intuitive scan deduced we had been eating donuts at the beach. She touched my chin and smiled, asking, "Did you have a good time?"

"I think so," I replied.

"What do you mean?" she said with a puzzled look on her face.

"Dad said I'm an old soul and that people will draw and talk to me... right dad?"

He turned and looked over his shoulder and said, "Close, luv. You are an old soul and people will be drawn to talk to you."

"George!" mom exclaimed. "You can't put that pressure on her. She's just a little girl."

Dad didn't respond or explain himself any further that evening.

As I went to bed, my head felt foggy. When I awoke, I went to tell my dad that I had dreamt of green trees and bright blue angels. He winked, walked to the counter to turn the kettle on and said, "We're going to England."

EGGS, BACON, AND SOVEREIGNTY

After we had settled into life in England, we made a small trip over to visit family in Wales. The first morning there, we awoke and walked downstairs for breakfast. Our relatives asked what we would like to eat. My brother and I looked at each other and said, "Eggs and bacon please!"

There was a moment of silence and then our relatives left for the market. While they were gone, dad sat us down and explained that those items were a luxury, a special breakfast and cost a "pretty penny."

I remember feeling nervous that we had offended our family and somehow as kids we were not worthy. Dad, reading my face, said, "It's okay. Edmondsons are generous hosts."

I had seen this growing up as my dad had ensured that everyone in our home was generously taken care of. Even if it was the last piece of bread we had, "it would always taste sweeter when shared," he would say.

Later in life, I explored my Celtic roots further, learning that Celtic tradition meant being generous hosts, sharing unconditionally, a virtue mirrored for hundreds of years in the sovereignty of the land. The tradition ran deeper than simply being generous with the things you had to share but being generous with your soul, your heart, your time, and your presence. It is an honored connection to the sacred generosity of the land and that you will always have what you need—abundance abounds when you care for the land.

I embraced this tradition completely and fostered a deeper appreciation for the origin of my family name, Edmondson, which translates as Prosperity-Protector.

Being generous, creating a welcome environment and reverence for the sacredness of home, seemed to come naturally to me, even at a young age. I could feel the voice of ancestors whispering "Aye luv, good job" when I embodied that essence. I wondered if this natural feeling was also what others felt and why they were "Drawn to me," as dad had said. Did my old soul "just know" how to create the invitation of hospitality akin to generations past?

SHE'S JUST A LITTLE GIRL—NOT ANYMORE

When I was eleven, my mom announced that she couldn't take the life we had been living. She wanted more stability and security. The gypsy lifestyle of traveling and living all around the world without a real plan in place, though much like her own childhood, was too much for her to bear any longer.

She made plans to find a job in San Francisco and would be traveling ahead of the family to get things set up. As she left, I felt a mix of anger, fear, pride, and awe. Here was a woman who had quietly played the role of mother and wife, floating from city to city, state to state, country to country, whenever my dad said so. She had left family and friends behind numerous times, doing her best to create the sacredness of home wherever we were.

No longer, though. She had had enough. She stood in her worth and said *no more*. Not only did she speak her truth but she acted on it.

Her Queen energy and voice echoed in my young ears for years to come.

On our final moving day, my dad, my brother, and I loaded up the van, getting ready to do the fourteen-hour drive from our home in Crescent City to San Francisco. We had been in Crescent City longer than anywhere else, and it felt like home. I was in tears. We left the simple farm life, surrounded by nature, with the ocean on one side and the redwoods the other. We had lived there long enough for me to have friends—real friends—and long enough to make it into multiple years of the yearbook—a big deal to me.

Just before locking up the house for the last time, I told my dad that I needed to use the bathroom. I went inside the house and, much to my dismay, I had started my moon menstrual cycle. No one had prepared me for this milestone. There were no words of wisdom, no loving presence of my mom, no supplies, no guidance. Nothing. I did what I could to clean up and sheepishly climbed into the moving van. I told my dad we needed to stop at the store. He glanced angrily at me and asked why. I explained, feeling the rush of pink heat fill my chest, neck, and cheeks as my kid brother looked at me in bewilderment and snickered.

My dad walked me to a neighbor's house, knocked on her door, and abruptly explained the predicament. She smiled kindly at me and took me into the house. She asked what I knew, and I knew nothing. She walked into the other room to talk with my dad and instructed him to go to the store for supplies. While he was gone, she called my mom and put me on the phone with her. As soon as I heard my mom's voice, I burst into uncontrollable tears. "Mom, I need you," I sobbed. She did her best to console me on the phone and explained that no one had really explained things to her either and she had learned by just watching how things went for her older sister.

During the half-day drive down the coast, a mix of feelings swirled within me. How could generations of women not talk about something they knew was going to happen? Why was I not important enough to have been prepared for this day? Why was my dad angry at me when I hadn't done anything wrong? *Had* I done something wrong? How could I be so angry at my mom and need her so deeply at the same time?

I felt utterly powerless, disconnected from my body, and unsure of who I was or who I was supposed to be. All I knew was that I was no longer "just a little girl."

LEAVING

After we arrived in San Francisco I realized just how ill-prepared I was for the transition. In Crescent City, we had farm life. I was a tomboy, content in my connection with nature and playing outdoors with my brother. We lived a humble and simple life.

In this new land, I was thrust into social rules I had no clue how to navigate. At school I saw how family dynamics were different for my classmates from what I was used to, money abounded and it didn't for us, and girls were girls, boys were boys. I didn't fit in, and some who noticed this reminded me of it daily. The bullying that I endured in the first couple of months of seventh grade was unbearable. I had no self-esteem, no self-worth. Desperately wanting to find a place to be welcomed, I slipped into valuing the approval of others over valuing myself.

One day in English class our teacher said we would be writing a book together. We would be published poets. This was our time to put pen to paper and freely express ourselves.

Panic rushed through my body. Could I really freely express myself? What would happen when I did? Would I be teased? Judged? Ostracized?

That evening I laid in bed and wondered if I had the strength to speak my truth. Memories of countless moments from my early youth when I had trusted my voice flooded me, while the voices of my ancestors whispered in my ears, "Aye luv, you do have the strength!"

The next day in class I penned,

"The ocean, waving its hand at the beach,
the beach awaiting.
People always in a rush, hurry by.
A little girl, remembering all the things
she had done:
collecting agates and shells on the beach,
hiking through the tall giant redwoods,
her house like a Swedish cottage,
and the yellow beach chairs on the redwood deck;
her cocker spaniel, Sandy, running round
and round the yard, playing with her cat,
Ebony; the open garden
with its green beans, radishes, and beets,
and the strawberries,
just waiting for a drink of water,
a ray of sun;
her horses running and resting in the backyard;
her tree house on an old elm tree stump;
the old row boat, and the daisies
throughout the yard ...
Gone.
She has to say good-bye
to the ocean and the beach.
She must go away and never come back,
but she will always remember her friends
from there, and as she turns to leave
with tears in her eyes, and goes
to a new and distant place,
all she has now are all of her memories
like the shells she collected
and put in a jar,
her feelings and memories
bottled up..."

After our poems were published in a collective book titled *Tools of the Universe*, we were each asked to read them to the class. As I stood, feeling the rush of pink heat fill my chest, neck, and cheeks, I fearfully read the words aloud, gaining strength with each stanza. When I took my seat I felt tears stinging my cheeks and couldn't bring myself to lift my head and look around the room.

At recess a couple of the girls and one boy came up to me and asked if we could hang out together. In that moment, a small cure for my sorrow was accessible. Through writing and speaking my truth, just as my brave mother had done in making this move, I could slowly reconnect to my worth, giving space for my self-esteem to blossom. I was hopeful this was the beginning of a beautiful new chapter.

IT ALL CAME CRASHING DOWN

After the summer of my twelfth birthday, my dad had a massive stroke. The doctors told my mom to prepare herself to be a widow. Fresh in all of the bold changes and leaps of faith, suddenly my family was facing dire circumstances without financial resources or support. The end result was a twelve-year journey of intense sacrifice, immense pain, and a deep imprinting of codependency on all of us.

The new and part-time job my mom had secured was now the sole income for the family, and my dad needed full-time care. At that time, we had no family, friends, or community to turn to. My mom sat me down and said she needed me to help out—in a big way—and that she knew that I could do it.

"I know you can," my dad said. "And what you don't know I trust you'll figure out."

This was said as if it was a fact and, like so many other things said to me before, I figured it had to be true, even if it didn't feel so.

I dropped out of public school, became my dad's primary caregiver, took care of the house, home-schooled myself, and helped my brother with his homework when he came home from school.

I was praised for being a fixer.
I was praised for being a caregiver.
I was praised for being a good girl.

When I asked for help, I was told "Figure it out—I know you can" or "Don't bother your mom, she's had a rough day."

I learned to say okay though inside I felt ill from swallowing the sourness of untrue words.

I struggled with being a good daughter who cared for her family while I wanted so much more.

I didn't know how to untangle myself from stories that were not mine and to release what was not mine to carry. I craved a different life. I felt deep longing for something other than my reality.

I was angry—Oh, so angry. And yet, I never showed this. I smiled a false smile and said, "I'm okay." I did everything that was asked of me, and I lost myself in the role of caregiver. I slipped farther and farther away from my sovereignty. I didn't know how to navigate healthy boundaries or relationships, and when I tried, it was messy and confusing.

My view of feminine and masculine expressions were limited and left me wanting. Every time something would fall apart at home, I would be sent in to fix it. Every time I battled with my parents for freedom or autonomy, I felt more and more alone and suppressed. I released all of myself into pleasing my family so as not to create waves in an already stressful situation. "Be a good girl, Deb."

One of my few solaces during this journey was my writing process. As I put pen to paper, I felt words older and wiser than my years pour from me. Generations of traumas, sufferings, and painful patterns deeply encoded on DNA, screaming out from inside, begging me to turn the sorrows into serenity and wounds into wisdom.

Near the end of my dad's life, he shared with me that he knew he was never meant to be on this earth for a long time. He told me that his family had lived rough and short lives and he truly felt alone, even in a crowded room. I listened tearfully as he poured out his heart to say he was sorry I had given up so much of my childhood. He asked, though, that I give up one more thing and follow the path of the family in spiritual matters. One of the hardest truths for me to speak came next. I told my dad that I had to follow the spiritual path that was true for me. I would always treasure the guidance he and mom had instilled in me... *and,* I needed to walk my own path, making my truth my own between me and my creator.

Weeks later, he slipped into a coma and never awoke. During his last hours on this earth, I sat by his bedside and poured my heart out, tearfully speaking all of my truths. My final words to him were, "Dad, you can pass in peace now. I promise to look out for mom and my brother. I'll be there for them. You don't need to worry. I love you. Your little copper knob is strong, an old soul, and I'll be okay. I know you'll always be by my side looking out for me."

As I walked into my apartment less than an hour later, my roommate ran up the stairs to tell me the hospital was calling to say that my dad had passed.

WOUNDS TO WISDOM

The decade after my dad passed was filled with countless experiences of settling, compromising, hurting, struggling, and walling myself off from connection for fear of being hurt. And when I did let my wall down, I often chose poorly, having insecurities that set my boundaries and limiting beliefs that guided my actions. To the untrained eye, I was living an exciting and vibrant life, but when the curtain was pulled back I was full of questions that ran deep, living a life that pushed me forward on a journey to be sensible, practical, and responsible in all areas of my life. I had lost time to catch up on all "the important life achievements" after all. Again, I had to sacrifice to succeed and follow a path that others prescribed for me.

Even amongst all of the codependent preoccupations with the happiness of others, there was this quiet yet strong voice inside me. It called out for healing, release, and meaningful connection.

Slowly, day by day, week by week, month by month, and year by year, I journaled my way to healing.

I explored counseling and spirituality that cracked a part of my soul open so the light could shine through for me to find my way to sovereignty.

I journeyed deep into feminine healing. I invested in myself and acknowledged my worth. I released old stories and broken beliefs. I listened to myself. I gave myself the space and sacred container to be heard, witnessed, and celebrated. I explored the depths of what brought me joy and aligned my actions only to those things, no longer doubting who I was or how to be in this world.

The whisper of my mom's Queen voice was subtly still in my ears. But now I could hear my own Queen voice. She said, "You are wise beyond your years and you have work to do. It's time to rise up. You were put on this earth to heal the intergenerational trauma and suffering of your family and guide others to the same healing."

As I did the work, my intuition became more accessible. My sovereignty became attuned, and an integral piece to my path clicked in.

I learned that a wonder woman with a full cup only doing what she joyfully said "yes" to is a universally different powerful force than a kickass woman struggling to live up to her "yes" from an empty cup.

I never imagined that the woman who I am today was possible, yet I intuitively always knew she was there. I now see the path that I am meant to travel and understand that everything I've ever done has led me to this point in the journey.

As a Spiritual and Intuitive Coach, **Deborah Harlow** focuses on the deep inner-child healing that is necessary for lasting transformation. She works with young girls, women, caregivers, and families.

Deborah's training in Psychology and Sociology laid the groundwork for her lifelong curiosity about people. As a young girl she was enthralled with wonder observing how individuals would engage with each other, nature, and themselves.

Early on in life, Deborah learned to listen to her intuition and allow her old soul to guide her. Her journey into becoming a youth caregiver at age twelve caused her to go into flight or flight response, where trauma took focus, silencing her intuition.

Caregiving for her father from age twelve to twenty-four, she lost connection to her truth and became completely removed from her sovereignty. After her father passed away, Deborah began a journey of healing which played a critical part in forging who she was always meant to be... an intuitive guide—a heart sherpa—who cares about creating meaningful connections so people can trust their truth, align their actions to their desires and create beautiful legacies.

Her journey to healing was so profound that she knew she was being guided to not only heal herself but break the karmic ties of intergenerational trauma so that she could help others experience the same profound healing.

Deborah deepened her capacity to serve by becoming a Certified Mediator in California, Certified Sistership Circle Facilitator, and Certified GirLife Facilitator. These trainings have added tools to her coaching "tool belt." Deborah creates safe containers that allow for the tough conversations to be had and the shadow work to be done.

As a highly sought after coach, public speaker, facilitator, and mentor, Deborah has learned to trust her truth, find joy in the journey, and take massive leaps of faith to share her experiences with others.

How might life have been different if there had been a place for *you* to be seen, heard, witnessed, and loved?

Imagine a space where you are held and supported. Imagine having time to tune in, time to reflect, and time to explore your truth. Imagine feeling clear, confident, and committed to your desires. Imagine no longer traveling the journey alone. This magical space exists in the work that Deborah does with her clients through one-on-one coaching, group coaching, workshops, and retreats.

Learn more about Deborah and her work at **www.TheJoyfulLeader. com, www.DeborahHarlow.com**, and on social media at **www.instagram.com/heartsherpa/**

Special Gift

DIVINELY ALIGNED YOU

A Journal for Creative Expression of Joy, Sovereignty, and Healing to Connect with Your Inner Wisdom

Access here:
https://mailchi.mp/thejoyfulleader/sovereign-unto-herself

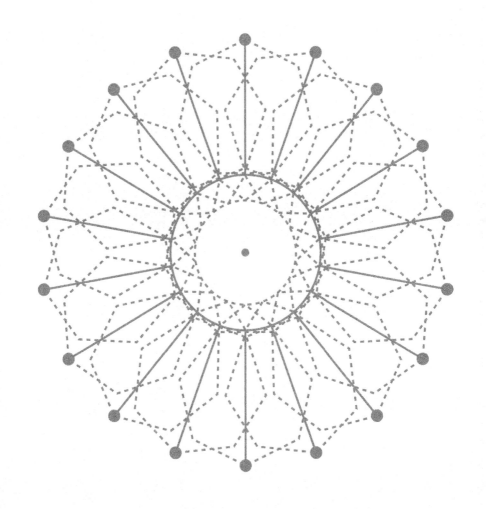

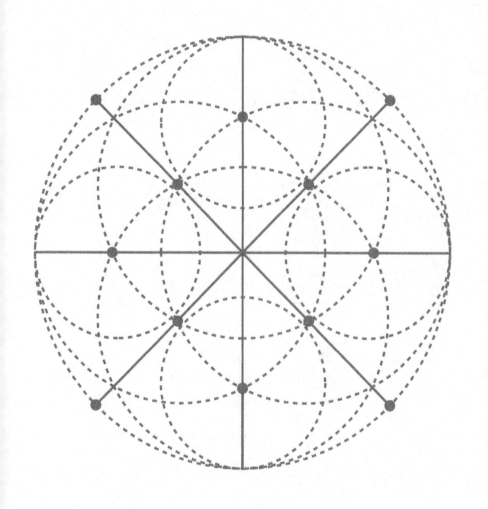

Emanating Love Undeterred

BY TAIDA HOROZOVIC

Thank you, Beloved, for seeing me through.
I love you, I trust you, I surrender to you.

Sitting in the unknown has come as medicine in a time that requires my highest trust, evolving inside the deep mystery of my heart... of all our hearts.

My life of roaming from place to place has left me craving a home beyond the temple I've cultivated within myself—and I found that home in love. Divine love homegrown from within and received through the universe inside of us and the universe out there. Abundant never-ending love that expands and activates us into the higher self in perfect alignment with our truth and purpose.

FOLLOWING MY HEART

My choices have been made following my heart. Though it doesn't always make life easier, choosing to follow my heart has affected the direction of my life greatly and given me a chance at a life of simplicity and beauty. I've experienced life-saving integration with my Self by reconnecting with my body, living in deep synchronicity with nature, releasing and transmuting a lot of my past, and coming into a new awareness and deeper love of my life, my body, and my path of personal evolution.

I felt the allure of the love that I am. I listened. I deepened into that activated divine feminine, a lovingly tended-to self-expression, and a playfully opened path to prosperity through a creative dance and embrace of inner muse in her alchemy. That's what opened the portal.

When I was able to focus on myself and sit still, I discovered amazing medicine through crystals—befriending many and holding rose quartz as a powerful guide, a friend of a familiar frequency that invigorated my sacred self-expression. While being in nature for hours on end, often in silence, I remembered the many languages that my soul speaks and underwent a luscious cell renewal that came naturally. I needed this. Taking the time to remain connected to nature is a lifeline to nurturing health and living the life that we desire.

Five years passed by, and I desired a more integrated life. With all the elements in my life that made that possible, I was able to spend a lot of time in stillness—in meditation, in nature, and on nature walks with my beloved. This was simply me being fully content and truly happy—a life of resonance in raised vibration.

Walking the path of love requires that we remain true to walking it and that we keep our gaze on that beautiful opening that offers deeper meaning to life—a source of new beginnings, energy, balance, and creative harmony. The aliveness that awaits us must first be embraced within us. And it's not all pretty.

HOLDING BACK

I was still holding myself back.

It wasn't intentional; in fact, I was on a clear path to be even more open-hearted and embrace all the new beginnings. And I was motivated to dim down my ego in every facet of my life, to notice the ego's wants creeping up, keeping it in check as I began to learn to surrender more, to humble down and humble down some more.

And it was working. At times, it was challenging and exhausting. But something unexpected happened. I began to see more fully through the eyes of my soul being—and through the eyes of the woman I was becoming. That was humbling and a priceless gift for which I am thankful.

Holding myself back—when all I wanted to do was to surrender—was an inevitable step in a direction that made it easier to dismantle my life and let go of the pieces that didn't fit. I needed only to trust and continue to walk the path. *Trust.* I was yet to learn that there is so much support available to every one of us in that space of trust.

A RETURN TO LOVE

I'm an introvert and a lot of what is required to live and succeed in the world requires going outside the comfort zone. But it has always been easy for me to tell those who matter to me, "I love you." Being sensitive is my strength. It is a powerful mystical gift and lives directly in touch with the vibration of all beings near and far. Sensitivity is an awareness of various frequencies before they even reach us. Sensitivity nests a lot of magic in my life and allows me to live deeper in my emotional body.

In my need to work to support myself and be independent, I had succumbed to feeling like I needed to be something different to survive. I felt like I needed to put my dreams aside to keep a job, stay focused, and deliver on my daily checklist of to-do items. I turned away from the call of my soul and tamed my passion for life.

A lot of my shadow work has been working through how I overthink things and will often wait for something to feel ripe and ready. And I also spent time loving the shadow of fear and hesitation into a transmuted plane—into letting it go and embracing the unknown. An old pattern of a survival tactic would rather rationalize than attune to my higher self and meet my desires. (I'm not judging myself here but noting it in the awareness and letting old stories like this one go.) Our desires drive us to thrive, and I lovingly escort the traces of old stories out of my realm, making room for what wants to be manifested.

Being free is an essential prerequisite for a life fulfilled. All I ever wanted was to be free, to travel, to laugh, to learn, to be of service to the world... and to surrender to the vibrance awaiting me. With my hippie anarchist stance, total surrender was difficult. Dismantling systems of oppression we're surrounded by, including patriarchy and fixated gender roles requires effort, and there was a shedding of the need for effort and for resistance. The old call of resistance was filled by a call to devotion to heal, to love the self into an immaterial soul grain of ever living light, and to choose the self and what had already been set into motion and catalyzed.

Surrendering in my heart was one thing, but speaking about my desires and claiming them was another. There was a major release happening—a return to love. I could see it in the clearing of my throat chakra and in the beautiful meditations, visions, gifts, and signs flowing my way. I was feeling alive in a new way, a living abundance in my own body. I was chanting, speaking clearly, painting, dreaming, and feeling a new embrace, warmth, and love and the notion that I needed to do nothing.

An orca says hi telepathically. I meet Isis above in the clear golden sky beyond and above the clouds, her wings so strong and divine—she is showing me endless plains ahead. I dance barefoot at dusk as an ancient priestess in a cobbled street in India. The song that I sing conjures up the presence of remembrance. I am anointed and in resonant presence, moving calmly and happy in my own temple of the rose quartz. It is a portal to love.

Source energy is always flowing through us. Love flows through us. We are part of a bigger energetic and formless body in this universe. I now have access to this eternal light of energy—the Source. It is always available to us, and there isn't much we need to do to access it except to *open... trust... breathe.*

If your ego mind starts to wander and pull you away from your inner knowing, you can shift your awareness and take the simple steps to regain your center and be back in your sovereign truth and voice.

Ten years ago, I wanted a life of stability and security. Today, I sit in the unknown and emanate love undeterred. I am willing to find my way back to the center, to stillness, and to balance. I find my way back to the Self that is aligned with her higher self, and anything she does is holding the intention of the highest good of all beings on our mother planet.

LOVE AS AN INITIATION

I am so deeply grateful to be in the place of possibility to imagine and live my life with a priestess path integrated, to see where it leads, totally trusting and loving the surrender. And it is in my complete joy and gratitude that I am stepping into the role of feeling into how to serve as I walk as love. I am curious and excited to see what shape and form it will take but also appreciating fully the light and shadow work this path invites me to dance with.

Steeping more fully into a sacred purpose-filled life invites me to integrate more sacred moments in relationships. It means taking up space and time, and that can feel unsteady and unfamiliar or trigger old wounds. Acknowledging that which arises without trying to fix anything can be therapeutic and can be a release of old narratives. It can be a loving way to make room for new narratives.

This is how I embrace my undeniable connection to the feminine, to the exploration of the seer of sacredness in everything through the eyes of the feminine. For I am the seeress of the feminine sacred. There is a kinship and a sense of belonging, of home that I have carried for lifetimes; it never goes away. This newness emerging is being witnessed also by our loved ones or those we are close to in our life. And it can be scary at times because of the beautiful unknown, the change of pace, the clearer intention of being on the path no matter what it may bring. The letting go of how things were in a sense. And this is uncomfortable.

On being uncomfortable: I've spent some time designing my life to be safe, comfortable, serene, and filled with nature and working hard to earn all of that. Now I am letting go of it all to step more fully into a new life of what was never before imagined, anticipated, or even spoken of. And that is a challenge. An initiation. An undoing in the making. It calls for taking off more layers to peel off any additional shadow that needs to be lovingly embraced so that alchemy can happen so that what needs to shine can. I am called to live life in observation of the joy, magic, colorfulness, playfulness, beauty, and love manifestation through sacred moments of truth. And so it is. I am a loving being, I walk in the magical world, I can hear the whispers of my heart, and I embrace all the vibrant colors that live within me.

My time spent in calm contemplation elevates my health, including my soul and spirit. In the times when we live with oversaturation of information and media, returning to the simple center of self may seem far away. And life's perceived circumstances can make us feel like we've been thrown for a loop. We never know what will happen. We can certainly be gentle and more loving to the self, settle down for a spell to really hear what our heart and body is telling us and embrace that truth as a possible way forward, as a heard message from within. It is that simple to honor our own body and soul. I offer to you sacred time for yourself, to breathe and hear the whispers from your innermost depth:

FULLY IN YOUR POWER

Personal alchemy can be reached so gracefully and naturally when time is dedicated to introspection and noticing the simplicity of independent spiritual work on self-love and oneness with the universe and the felt embrace of belonging. Neither a miracle nor a magic wand waved to make change, it is our conscious choice to embody change by loving the self into a new level of knowing. It is an experienced learning that begins with the intention to actually feel into that which is attempting to speak to us. Whether it is through our body's discomfort or emotional suffering, a bigger story wants to be woven and it begins with us listening. It begins with us taking the time to shift from doing to feeling, from managing to connecting, as we emerge more synchronized with the soul path, which brings more energy, more joy, and more purpose. It's like choosing to eat fresh, natural food over processed food and finding that fuel full of life force energy.

One of my favorite things to do is to spend time in the woods. I am in awe of the ancient wisdom of trees, and their knowledge transports me to new levels of understanding myself, accepting myself, and accepting other people, remembering I am a multidimensional being. Being near the trees is feeling the expansiveness of the heart through being in sync with the light and energy flow with our Pachamama. Feeling centered and not overwhelmed. Feeling expansive and not crowded by everyone's thoughts, needs, and wants. In this harmonious cycle of sitting with nature through conversations with trees, being in their midst, a new language was born for me—a language I remembered because it was a language of my gifts. The gift to manifest that which is within. The gift to express creatively that which is aliveness within me. And the gift to curate beauty as a way to honor each beautiful soul.

I came out of the unknown and for more than eight months, I've been making mandalas with flowers and crystals. My favorite is a mandala made and left in nature—in a field, near a tree, at the beach. And sitting in the unknown is where mandala emerged mostly indoors and as an expression of simple gratitude to love. An intention. A dedication. A poem. A prayer. It is for you, Beloved.

MAKE YOUR MANDALA

Are you feeling called, Beloved, to spend time with your sacred beautiful heart, to hear the call and whispers of your soul guiding you? Do you crave gentleness and simple love through color and natural elements? Are you in need of a grounding practice that will hug you back into the center of your heart, relaxing you fully so you can sit in your sovereign seat of your unique perfect frequencies? You are always welcome here.

Mandala is a Sanskrit word for "circle." It represents "as within, so without." I think of mandalas as beautiful pieces of art that reflect the soul's song. They can be an altar, a prayer, or an affirmation. They can be your witness, living art, and most importantly, a mandala is a freeing expression of your higher-self frequency, your divine self.

I usually light a candle and take a few breaths first. I might put my hands on my heart.

And then I listen. If you feel called to be still in pause, you may be hearing the call.

Feel into what wants to come through. What does it sound like? Is it a word, a color, a feeling, a scent, a sound? This is your intention.

As you feel deeper into the intention and perhaps gaze at or near the candle (you may feel that you want to keep your eyes closed), feel into the elements that are calling you and begin to gather them or make a list for later. The elements can be anything that feels right for you: shells, flowers, fruits, vegetables, spices, dried fruit, twigs, crystals—something that feels like a natural piece collected directly from Mama Gaia after she discards it. Once you've gathered your pieces, clear the surface on which you will create your mandala. She will tell you the colors, shapes, and elements she wants to come through.

Say your intention silently, or out loud if that feels right, and do so near the candle. Put your hands over your heart and feel the colors and the shape of your mandala coming alive as you think of your intention.

Feel the mandala arise. Feel it emerge gently within you.

Begin to put the pieces together as you create your mandala. It might be a circle mandala. Or it might be a spiral or a triangle. This is especially true if you are feeling called to do crystal grids or to explore sacred geometry.

A mandala is merely an unambitious reflection of your beautiful soul.

There is no right or wrong. Whatever you create will be beautiful and perfect as is the intention you set that works for your own wellness, or perhaps it is for the wellness or protection of others.

Once your mandala is complete, you may want to take a photo of it and share it with others.

There are no rules, and mandala is not made to last long. Feel into when she is ready to be released back to Mother Earth. It might be a day or two or three. It might be a few hours. Your mandala reflects the perfect art piece that you are and your soul's longing to express her song.

Thank you for listening to the call of your heart, Beloved. You are love and you are free through love.

Taida Horozovic is on her Priestess Path to Walk As Love. A communications professional for over twenty years, Taida loves helping organizations thrive.

As a nomadic soul, she is happiest when she's outdoors, near trees, and taking pictures in nature. Most recently, her inspiration is writing poetry, mandala-making with flowers, and deepening into which crystals resonate with her light-and-shadow-qualities-work.

She is a plant-based diet enthusiast and loves to travel.

Connect with Taida at **taida.horozovic@gmail.com** and **instagram @tainomadica.**

Special Gift

SACRED MANDALA ART

Receive a pdf full of beautiful photography—colorful flower mandalas—part of a sacred creative and meditative practice from Taida Horozovic.

Access here: **https://bit.ly/2TA1vYk**

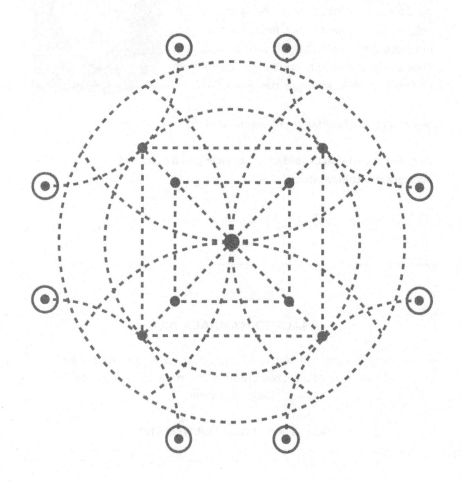

Traveling the Path of Solitude to Find My True Voice

BY RINA LIV

......⌐℘⌐......

I have always been alone—though, I see now, that I wasn't really ever alone. God was there.

As a baby in Cambodia, I was abused by my step-grandmother. She was supposed to watch me while my mother, her stepdaughter, worked the rice fields. But she hated her daughter, and used me as a weapon to try to hurt my mother. My step-grandmother took her rage out on me by repeatedly burning me in the belly with incense. However, what that callous old woman didn't realize was that my own mother didn't love me enough to care! For so much of my life, when I looked at my scars, I felt the sting of not having had my own mother's love.

We all want love. Some of us, like me, grab onto the closest thing we can find to what love looks or feels like. Sometimes it's just a toxic impostor. That was the case for me the first forty-eight years of my life. I always wanted what I did not have or could not have. I tried to grab hold of what I wanted with all my power, and for decades, I repressed painful memories. But ultimately, I had to face the truth so as not to destroy myself. I had to face my past in order to open the door to my future.

My family came to the United States from Cambodia in the winter of 1975, poor immigrants displaced by war. I came with my father, mother, two brothers, and step-grandfather. We came with nothing and didn't speak the language. My father worked two full-time jobs to provide for us. After just three years in the States, he had saved enough money to buy a house for us. He was the only positive example in my childhood.

By the time I was five, my mother was abusing me physically, mentally, and emotionally. I was always made to feel as if I was nothing and that I would amount to nothing. I was never good enough for her no matter what I did or how much I tried. And I spent what feels like my whole life trying to prove her wrong and earn her love.

But even as she beat down my spirit, my God gave me strength to lift up my head and know that I was His child and loved by Him. God's love kept me going when I was that scared little girl left alone and vulnerable to abuse by those who were supposed to care. With no adult protecting me, I learned to protect myself. I was stubborn—and strong.

When my mother beat me, I refused to let her see me cry no matter how much it hurt. That would anger her even more and she would beat me more; then, once alone in my room, I would cry out in pain. I would pray and ask God, "Why? What did I ever do to deserve such treatment from my own mother?" I would pray for God to either take her life or take mine. But I knew He had a purpose for me and that I was here for a reason. My heart, somehow, remained soft.

One day at age five, when we had been in the United States for about a year, I was on the couch napping after school. The couch was by the window, the sun shining in, and as I woke up, there was a dark figure over me. When my eyes adjusted to the brightness, I saw it was my step-grandfather. He pulled off my pants and laid on me, and I felt pain and confusion. When he was done with me, he told me that this was our secret; I could never tell anyone because my mother would be very angry at me. I kept the secret, and the sexual abuse went on until I was eleven years old.

Even in my adult years, when my mother could no longer abuse me physically, the emotional, mental, and verbal abuse continued. I struggled, trying to be the good daughter who loved and honored her mother, but how could I when she was such an evil person? My mother had always controlled who I could have as friends. I had been sheltered from Western culture and forbidden to have friends outside our Cambodian community. Yet I didn't know how to break free from all the pain.

Finally, in 1990, at age eighteen years old, I joined the Army. I hoped for a better life and liberation from my mother's control. I wanted a normal life, one where I could learn to trust and to love. I set out on this journey alone and wondered if I would ever be loved or wanted by someone... My mother had told me repeatedly that I would never amount to anything... was she right? I was willing to take a chance because success would be the best revenge!

By joining the Army, I was exposed to Western culture—a rude awakening! I was naive and had so much to learn. I may have been living in the United States, but I was certainly brought up with traditional Cambodian beliefs. I felt lost and trapped between two cultures, not really belonging in either one. I had to learn who I was and somehow interweave those two cultures together. After my discharge from the Army, I had a much stronger mind, but I still had a lot of learning and growing to do to fully become the real me.

I called my mother and told her that I was not coming back home. I planned to start my life over as far away from her as I possibly could. But she cried and begged me to come home and said that she had changed. My soft heart and genuine hope for the best in people allowed me to believe her. I returned home—a decision that I would soon regret.

The day after I got home from getting discharged from the Army, I went to the mall for an eye exam at Sears. A young man at Sears was returning some tools. He approached me and we started talking. He asked me to go to the movies with him that day and I agreed. We became friends and he would come over to my house and visit or pick me up to go somewhere. My mother for some reason had liked him a lot. She told me that I should marry him because he was a good man. I wasn't ready for marriage—I just wanted to go to college, live my life, and figure out who I was. But somehow she talked me into marrying him. We married for all the wrong reasons, and I came to feel trapped in a loveless marriage.

Over the years my husband's temper worsened, and he behaved much like a toddler, getting angry with people, cursing at them and throwing things. Sometimes I had to literally sit on him so he wouldn't do anything stupid! During the last decade of our marriage, he became more verbally, emotionally, and mentally abusive. As he saw it, everybody else was to blame for his mistakes. I grew so tired of his accusations and verbal abuse that one morning I woke up and told myself I'd had enough.

Throughout my whole life, I was always living for other people and protecting them. But now, I wanted to live for myself and be free from all forms of abuse. I was physically, mentally, emotionally, and spiritually drained. I had nothing left in me and was exhausted. I had lost myself and my identity, first with my mother and then with my controlling husband. I was always trying to fix my mother or my husband but then I realized that I couldn't fix them; the only person I could change was me. I needed to sever the cords that tied me to those who hurt me. I had to learn to have my own voice.

So I divorced him.

After my divorce, I continued to work on myself. Abuse, neglect, shame, loneliness, self-doubt, emotional chaos, and guilt were the themes of my life that had to be rewritten. I learned to let go of all that suffering rather than let it define me.

Of course, I failed. I had been trying to heal myself by myself, but I couldn't do it alone. I needed God. I read scriptures in the hopes of finding answers on how to fix my broken soul. Through scriptures, God revealed so many people who had failed because they relied on their own strength. I realized that I had to surrender it all to Him for the healing to begin.

My life had been filled with expectations of success and a perfect life with a perfect family. But no matter how hard I tried, I continued to fail. I gave and gave to those toxic relationships until finally, everything within me was depleted. So I had to learn to establish boundaries, protect myself, and begin healing.

I blocked out all the negative people from my life. I looked deep within myself and searched my soul to see where I needed healing. I stayed strong in my belief that I could change. I had to learn to forgive the people who had hurt me and to see them, too, as broken and in need of healing. It has been a long and painful journey and I am still on this journey toward healing—but it is so worth it.

Truthfully, even though I felt like God had abandoned me at times, He never left me. He had worked on me and molded me and taught me to love, to have faith, to be patient, to have compassion with others, and to not judge myself or other people. He kept my heart soft. God was there as a I dug and excavated through the dirt of shame, guilt, and suffering. He was there as I found my voice and my sovereignty.

My past sexual abuse had left me unable to conceive children. But, after my marriage ended, I went to Cambodia on a mission trip and met five beautiful children. A year later, I went back and adopted all five of them. God had promised me that I would have children, and I held on to that promise for decades. When I finally stopped trying to control the situation on my own, He worked His miracles. What men meant to do for evil, God used for His good. I had believed I was "damaged goods," but God taught me otherwise—I was saved and redeemed from my own beliefs of unworthiness. I could now be the mother I always wanted to be, and I could give my children—and myself—the unconditional love we all deserved.

I returned home from my third mission trip to Cambodia in November of 2019. On this trip, I had tried to bring my eldest two daughters to the United States to be with me. I had attempted to adopt them—or even just sponsor them—to come live with me in the United States but I was unable to, as the United States had closed adoption from Cambodia because of child sex-trafficking and the lack of prevention from the Cambodian government. I talked with an attorney and was told that I could not sponsor the girls because we were not blood-related and they were both under 30-years-old—a red flag. I was told my option was to bring them to the United States by getting them each a student visa and enrolling them in college full-time. Unfortunately, I couldn't afford to bring them home and pay for two college tuitions—especially as foreign students. The doors were closed and my heart broken as I told my two daughters that I could not bring them home with me. That's when I prayed and decided that I was going to open a medical clinic and orphanage in Cambodia one day—so that I could move there and be with all of my children.

For now, I support them by paying for their education and providing them with the basic and essential necessities. Even though it's not ideal, I wouldn't trade it for one second!

Life has taught me some hard lessons, but through the power of God's love and my own resilience, my heart is open and I am now the sovereign queen of my Queendom. I unapologetically claim my power and my voice. I love myself, and my five adopted Cambodian children—no matter where we are. And, finally, I am at peace and in gratitude for the beauty of life. I know my purpose, and I am here to serve with love.

Special Gift

Rina would love to hear *your* story!

Reach out and connect by emailing her at
rinanurse@hotmail.com

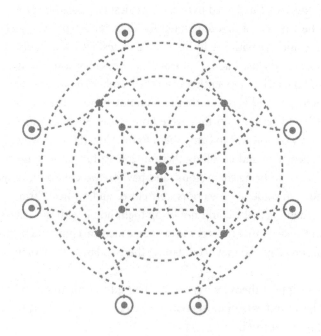

Rina Liv is a traveling nurse practitioner working in the field of addiction medicine. Having endured a lifetime of physical, sexual, and emotional abuse in silence, her sacred work is to share hope with others who have suffered from abuse and have turned to drugs or alcohol to numb their pain or forget their past.

Rina's dream is to show and spread God's love by opening a medical clinic in her birth country of Cambodia that provides free medical care for those in need. In partnership with fellow Flower of Life Press author Alis Mao, Rina intends to make this dream possible and help the people of Cambodia, many of whom continue to suffer from the genocide that was experienced in the 1970's.

While on a mission trip to Cambodia, Rina fell in love with five children, whom she adopted a year later. Rina is able to provide financial support and visits Cambodia as much as possible to share in their lives. Her oldest daughter, in college, is majoring in IT information technology. Her second oldest daughter plans to attend college and become a designer.

Despite her painful past, Rina is optimistic about love! She trusts that a man of strong faith who loves God and who has a heart to serve others will find his way into her life! A foodie at heart, she enjoys going to restaurants, cooking, and entertaining friends. She lives in Oregon and enjoys hiking, traveling, and visiting wineries.

Rina began writing as part of her own healing process. Her memoir, "Traveling the Road of Solitude: Discovering My True Self" will be published in 2020 by Flower of Life Press.

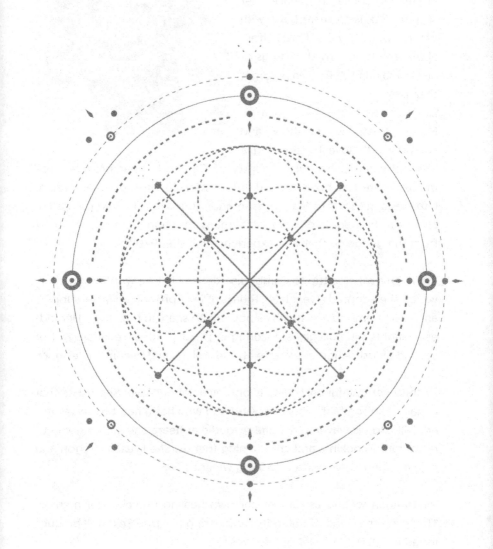

Claim Your Crown

BY MICHELLE ORWICK

This is a conversation with the Goddess of 10,000 Names—as channeled and interpreted by Michelle Orwick

Hello, my beloved. I am often called Great Mother.
I walk with and dwell within you.
My message is this: Share your story of greatness.
It is a call to reawaken your divine sovereignty.

THE SEARCH

Beloved, you are on a journey of self-discovery, searching to embody the *frequency* of love... to recognize that love *is* the frequency of your sovereign self.

Yet, too often, you feel empty or as though you are losing yourself.

Some days, you forget who you have been, who you are, and who you can be.

You are not lost, daughter.
You are safe.
Remember that you are blessed.

It is time to break the chains of old identities that weigh you down like an anchor; forgive yourself for the should haves, the would haves, and the could haves.

It is your birthright to love and be loved; it is your power to heal your wounded heart through the process of forgiveness.
Forgiveness heals all wounds.
The Divine Sovereign knows this.

To move past fear and worry, take action. Use the violet flame to burn doubt.

Step into your power; activate your birthright. Grow and expand.

The time is now, beloved.
The time has come to reawaken;
for the veil of mystery and magic is reopening.

TRUE LOVE

Young girls dream of being a princess and being rescued by the prince.

However, my dear one, love is not as it has been defined this way—with these old myths and fairytales.

Love is much more than you understand.

It's more than the tiara placed upon your princess head.

It's more than the ring slipped upon your finger—symbols that give perceived worth and value.

There is only true love.
This true love lives within.

This outward search causes the pain of disconnection and the illusion of separation... separation from your Inner Beloved, your divine birthright of true love—the love that you truly are.

......⌇⌇......

THE PATH TO THE INNER BELOVED

The path begins with a vow, a sacred commitment to treat yourself as the Divine; to treat yourself as you would the Goddess.
When you take this vow, answering the call from your sacred self, then you will find the love that has been awaiting you all along.

You are awakening.
It is time to embrace your innocence.
It is time to reawaken the seeker within you and reclaim your wonder.
It is time for you to make a choice.

Along this path, you begin to acknowledge that you are a powerful, expansive being of light. A Creatrix.

From this place of understanding, you realize life offers a series of lessons that do not happen *to* you, but *for* you.

As you remember that you carry and create things in the womb—this is the life force substance—what you want and desire become completely available to you; however, if you have a speck of doubt, it will withdraw all of your manifesting power.

What will you choose?

When you anchor your Inner Creatrix's power, you begin to heal—as that is your soul's mission.

At times, you'll feel the density of negative emotions holding you hostage from the future you are creating and from the present that you are experiencing.

As a Creatrix, you have the choice to work like an artist with paint or clay, or like a writer creating her story.

Your choice is your initiation.
An initiation requires getting comfortable with the unknown. Once you surrender the unknown, you can share your love freely from your heart, entering the gateway of receiving.

Fear of the unknown and resistance to surrender takes you away from your heart.

True Love is all about the heart.
You can welcome, within your body and within your field, perfect love and perfect trust. A prayer to find wholeness within yourself. To balance and recalibrate to the energy of divine love.

This is who you already are, and who you have been.

What will you choose?
Will you choose to see life as the initiation?
Will you surrender to receive your Inner Beloved?

CLAIMING YOUR CROWN

When you surrender to receive your true beloved and come into sacred union with yourself, the crown on your head becomes yours.

It can only be placed there by the self-mastery of thought, action, and deed. This is the crown of knowledge, leadership, and mastery.

Now, decide to know deep in your heart that this crown is something you are worthy of, that you deserve, and that you are to wear by divine birthright.

Your true crown is one that you must place upon your head with full authority.

Remember:
You are whole and holy.
You are love.

Beloved, practice kindness on yourself.

Practice feeling what it feels like to be whole.

Then allow yourself to dive into the waters of the initiatory unknown and claim your sacred union with your sovereign, crowned self.

Michelle Orwick—Twenty years a spiritual seeker, I have been a teacher and student for the last decade. My goal is to help people find joy in their lives, enabling the release of fear, worry, stress, and/or negativity. With that endeavor, I became a Reiki Master in 2010, and started absorbing all forms of magickal and metaphysical learning, delving into the study of world religion and how the brain is wired.  From there, I discovered ThetaHealing®, became an instructor in 2011, and earned the highest accommodation in the field with the Certificate of Science / Instructor in 2012. Acknowledging how it could change the neuro-pathways of our minds—enabling a new process and ability for someone to find their own way back to wholeness—I have in that time certified over 200 students and have offered over a thousand one-on-one healing sessions with my clients.

I have dedicated my life to guiding people on their spiritual journeys, helping them to create the life they desire, filled with joy and purpose. I specialize in helping clients to understand their truths, heal emotional shock and trauma from life events, and illuminate their path for future growth. My desire to serve and assist those who are on such a healing journey brought to birth a healing and educational center in Orlando, the **Odyssey Institute of Healing Arts**, a physical and online platform for education and guidance to those seeking awakening.

My path forward will lead those I serve on a path of manifestation delivered through meditation, teaching, and guidance to work within the law of attraction, creating the change of perception and mindset that alters reality and enables the desired life of purpose and meaning.

Learn more at **www.MagicalMichelle.com.**

Special Gift

CONNECT TO LOVE MEDITATION

Sign up for Michelle's Newsletter to receive her free "Connect to Love" Meditation.

Access here:

https://odysseyinstitute.kartra.com/page/Connect2Love

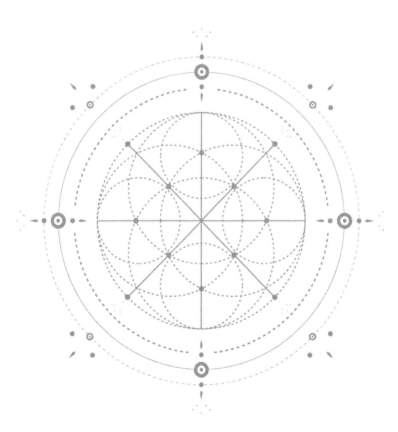

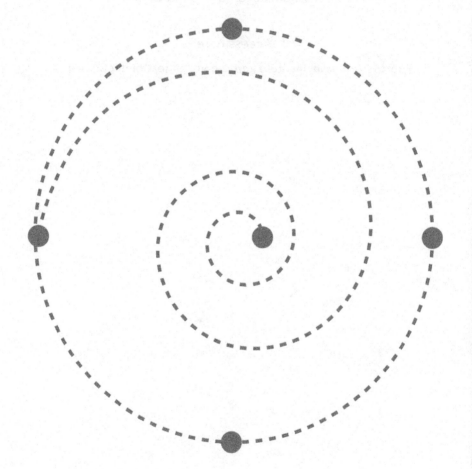

Reclaiming My Birthright to Sovereign Power and Joy

BY ELSA PEREZ DEAN

Welcome, Daughter
Take root
Feel the flow of life
Moving upward from the depths
Like a coiled snake unraveling,
Shedding old skin
In a luminescent golden ray of light
Expansive and powerful
Connecting you from below
And above
Welcome home, dear one
Take this gift as you soar.

—TRANSMISSION AT TEOTIHUACAN, MEXICO, 2019

Tears streamed down my upturned face as the warmth of the sun high above enveloped me. There, on my sovereign throne, I connected to a place both outside myself and within that anchored and expanded me across time and space. I felt a wholeness that can only be described as a homecoming, rooting me to my Essence Self in a way that I had longed to feel my entire life. I was Home. I was free.

I received this gift as I sat at the top of the Pyramid of the Sun in the ancient city of Teotihuacan, just north of Mexico City. This trip was nothing short of a miracle.

For much of my life, I lived in a deep-seated pattern of giving my "self" away for the sake of pleasing others. I wasn't even aware that I was operating in this way. I was so driven to please and be validated for all that I was giving.

I didn't notice how each time I swooped in to please, to rescue, or to be the responsible one, I was actually losing my sense of self. I was seeking love and worth outside of myself and, as a result, I was giving away my power. From this place, I struggled with feelings of resentment and disconnection to my creative fire, joy, and sovereignty.

How could I be my fully expressed self and still feel loved while standing in my power? How could I honor my own heart while honoring others?

Living to please others, with an aching need to feel externally validated, left me feeling empty. I longed for a sense of belonging and being seen that went beyond my own family. No amount of praise or validation would ever be enough. How could it? There was so much more beneath the surface to unearth and tend to.

I was often told I appeared strong, confident, and determined. I embodied masculine qualities as a way to mask my pain and sadness. Yet beneath that protective armor, there was a sensitive and intuitive being that had been hidden away. She was not to be trusted. I lived in fear and shame that I'd felt my entire life yet couldn't explain. I couldn't yet see how living my life to fit other people's ideas of who I should be, or relying solely on my masculine traits, was robbing me of my full essence. My innocent heart couldn't yet break the spell of shame from lifetimes long passed that were holding me back from standing in my sovereignty. This half-lived life was costing me my joy and my health.

Yet something inside pulled and guided me forward as if through dense fog.

Reflecting back now at my struggle to be seen—to find worth outside of myself and to compensate for feeling ashamed—there was also a wellspring of knowing within that filled me up. With no way to describe this or anyone to confide in, I simply ignored this aspect of myself for a long time.

I was asked once to recall the childlike joy and delight at the discovery of the world through innocent eyes. This request brought me to tears because I simply didn't have any memories of that magical little one. I could not access her joy. I began to realize that much of my life had been lived in the shadow of guilt, fear, and unspoken shame—not mine but of my ancestors. So much so that I no longer believe that joy even existed within me. As a child, I was told—no, I was directed—to be quiet or how to behave. I was told how to *be* and what to *do*. Joy was told to be quiet, and power was locked away. My little one was told to play quietly, to not create a disturbance.

But what if my life has been to create a disturbance? To break patterns that no longer serve? What if my whole life has been about reclaiming my birthright to the power and joy that were hidden away when I was a child? What if I am here to inspire others to reclaim their birthright? And if so, at what cost?

Much of my young life, there was little room to trust in the notion of joy for good. Instead, I believed that there would be a considerable cost if I showed up in my truth or expressed myself. I felt torn between the love that I felt in my heart and how conditioning had seeded a deep-rooted belief that I couldn't trust anyone, let alone my own inner compass or power.

I was born in San Francisco to parents who came from Mexico to create a better life. That is another story for another time. My story begins in the middle... in the gray area that is not entirely of this country or of theirs. In this middle, I felt the exclusion by kids in school and the teasing that I endured for being different despite living in one of the most culturally diverse cities in the world. In this middle, I felt the disconnection from my Mexican roots and my ancestors as my parents worked hard to adopt this country as our home. Whenever we visited family in Mexico, I felt the shame of privilege of being born in the U.S. and the guilt of the oppressed and the oppressor. I was born in between the boundaries and in between the worlds—at the cusp of a dark moon.

Painfully shy, and afraid to be myself for reasons I couldn't have begun to understand, I felt lonely and disconnected everywhere I went. The gift of loneliness was the time spent in my inner landscape imagining worlds full of beauty, magic, and wonder. In my imagination, anything was possible. I felt empowered and free.

In second grade, while in the library of my Catholic school, I discovered the mysteries of ancient Egypt and Greece quite by accident—or divine intervention, perhaps. I was suddenly transported to worlds beyond my small existence. I'd lose myself in myths and fairy-tales, feeling the words speak a secret language to my heart that felt both special and confusing. I was a voracious reader, and I felt connected to something I couldn't explain.

This introduction into the mythic journey was the tiny opening my young soul needed. Later, I was drawn to astrology even though the people I trusted considered it foolish. I became fascinated with learning everything I could about oracles, seers, and anything to do with magic. Despite the fact that the Mexican culture is filled with mysticism, my family dismissed much of it as nonsense. I continued to hide.

Yet the Mystery had a hold on me, and a part of me was open to receive.

Beyond my growing fascination with mysticism, astrology, and other worlds, I experienced moments of awakening that, even then, felt like deep remembrance. When I was eleven, I was visited by my Abuelo in my bedroom only to learn he had just passed away in Mexico. As a teenager, I often felt the presence of spirits in unexpected places. Vivid dreams opened me up to an expanse of infinite connection. Yet I continued to hide these truths from anyone for fear I'd be ridiculed by my family.

My Abuelita was a beacon of light in my life. She was a force to be reckoned with and a bit unpredictable. When my mother was ten, my Abuelita suffered a traumatic brain injury after falling out of a moving car onto the highway. After the injury, her life and mind were broken open. Medically, she'd been diagnosed as a manic-depressive schizophrenic, but our family often called her crazy. What I remember most about her now was her vivacious laugh and shameless expression of who she was in the moment. I saw her as fully alive, even on the many medications she was prescribed. She showed me what it looked like to live in the moment, to be fully expressed and unashamed. To me, that was intoxicating. But, seeing how our family responded to her was also terrifying.

As I grew older, I became filled with anger and resentment. I felt trapped and caged in my own life. I was ungrounded—not rooted in my essence—having hidden my true self away as a means of self-preservation. By then, I had moved to another state to forge my own life, had married, and was living the American dream, without feeling like I measured up to the dream. I continued to struggle with the truth of what I felt in my heart over the desire to feel needed and loved. I was caught in a spiral, living my life in an attempt to be seen outside of myself and for others to validate my worth. Yet, I also felt the desire to stand in my own power. I felt split as if I was two people—one angry, the other pure love—still unrooted and disconnected.

Becoming a mother in my thirties opened a portal within my heart. I felt a connection of deep remembrance to ancient feminine wisdom. Love cracked me open to hear with my heart once again and to slowly reclaim my sovereignty. Still, I didn't trust what I was feeling.

My son became the center of my life. His light—and pain—became a sacred mirror that awakened the innocent child within me. I was being called into union with my Divine Feminine heart. I was feeling both the strength of the Sacred Masculine within and a sense of deep shame of the feminine within me. Motherhood—and my connection to the Divine Mother—was calling me back to Mexico into a deeper relationship with my ancestors and the mysticism that had been lost through my family—back into a remembrance of my essence.

Despite this deep yearning, I didn't trust the whispers. I continued to force myself to buy into a life that wasn't genuinely mine and to ignore my heart, still seeking validation for my worthiness as a member of this larger tribe and still feeling like I wasn't enough. The more unworthy I felt, the more I pushed to gain validation—and the more I succeeded. My inner wisdom was trying to speak to me, yet I continued to avoid Her and to mistrust Her.

Until she finally got my attention in a big way.

My life unraveled with the news of a second pregnancy on my thirty-eighth birthday. At that point, my life had been quickly spiraling out of my perceived control. My marriage was barely hanging by a thread, my work life was depleting my soul, and I was lost. My initial response to the pregnancy was one of anger. With the intensity of my anger came a softening of my heart. As soon as I embraced the notion of new life growing inside of me and the chance to embrace this new soul, she left my body.

Devastated, I allowed shame and guilt to envelop me and take me into the darkness. As I entered into this dark period—to die to my old life—my body shut down. I was hospitalized for five days in an attempt to diagnose my inability to move my legs. She had forced me to stop. To listen. To reconnect to parts of myself that I had long ignored.

On the fourth day of my hospital stay, in a moment of lucid awareness, I became aware of a formless presence surrounding me. I was held in a love so pure, my heart burst open, and the tears released. I was in Mother's loving embrace. I heard Her whisper that it was time to let go of all the illusions. It was time to live my life in alignment with my power and joy. There was no escaping what She was asking of me and the changes I would have to make. Suddenly, I was more afraid of living and making those changes than I was of dying. I felt her arms envelop me closer, soothing me. I felt incredibly peaceful, knowing this was a gift and an awakening. I vowed to Her that if I could go home, I would make the changes being asked of me despite the immense fear and uncertainty this would entail. I was ready to honor this life.

The next day, the doctors sent me home. They could find nothing medically wrong with me despite my genuine physical symptoms. Told to go home and heal, I was being given a chance to reclaim my life, my joy, and my power.

Two years later, still slowly unraveling the illusion of my life, my husband, son, and I traveled to Mexico to visit my sister-in-law in Cuernavaca, where she was attending a work conference. This would be my first time back in Mexico in more than a decade and the first with my husband and son. The portal was opening.

During our stay, we visited a museum that had formerly been a palace. There, I came upon a mural by Diego Rivera titled "Crossing the Barranca." The moment I laid eyes on it, I instantly connected to the depth of my ancestors' pain. I felt it in my core. At forty years old, I was questioning every aspect of my life. Reflected in this mural was a montage of persecution, pain, and confusion that, up to that point, had no real context to my life experience. But this pain was in my bones and encoded in my DNA. As my eyes took in the story of the mural, I understood the origin of the shame that I'd felt for so long. I also felt the wholeness of the larger story being reflected in the eyes of the oppressed and the oppressor. The mural had been commissioned by an American ambassador in the former palace of Hernan Cortes, the Spanish conqueror of Mexico, and the irony was not lost on me. I am both American and Mexican. Both Indigenous and European blood course through my veins and inform my dreams and pain. I felt the love of the Mother envelop me once again, inviting me to see the whole image with my heart.

That trip was the beginning of the end of my life as I had known it.

The connection to the Divine within me had been reawakened and could no longer be ignored. She was asking me to choose love. To be in my power in the face of so much pain, inviting me to soften and forgive. She's been with me throughout the entire journey as I've slowly shed pieces of my old life to embrace the one I'm meant to live. Breaking these deeply ingrained patterns and wounds has taken a decade of seeking, undoing, and immense faith, compassion, and forgiveness. Breaking the spell of shame, of unworthiness, and of guilt has become my work for my heart and the One Heart.

Every choice I have made since that trip has led me here to the seat of sovereignty in love. At every choice point, I've come back to the still point within my heart, and the Divine within, to guide me.

There have been difficult choices to make such as leaving my career in search of a more heart-centered way to offer my gifts. Or the decision to fight for and ultimately end the marriage, which was no longer holding my husband and me in love. The Mother has been with me always.

Trusting in the Mystery and surrendering into uncertainty as part of a greater unfolding has opened my heart to forgiveness and more love for myself and all aspects of my life even in the face of these difficult times. The choice to remain open to love and forgiveness also allowed me to drop my protective shields and reunite with my husband from a place of sacred union.

Honoring each heart-centered whisper from sacred sovereignty has led me to another teacher as a sacred mirror who has inspired me, challenged me, and motivated me to listen to my heart and stand in my power as a Divine child of Love and Light. My heart is open and willing to see myself reflected in the other.

Each choice has been an invitation to step more fully into the seat of my power—a power that originates in Love. Her whispers continue to lead me on this path of Devotion as a daughter of the Divine, honoring all the wisdom that flows through me in service to beauty, joy, and the power of love. She called me home, back to Mexico and the Pyramid of the Sun, back to my essence self and my purpose.

My soul's purpose has been to create a disturbance and reawaken my somnambulant heart—to release the guilt and shame of my ancestors, both the oppressors and the oppressed. I am here to bring awareness of the Divine in each of us and to our connection to the one heart. There is no separation— only love and choice. All the rest is an illusion to keep us separated.

My life is directed by an innate knowing. When I look back on each choice I've made, no matter how challenging or rewarding, all were catalysts that began with a deep trust for what I knew to be true in my heart.

Each moment has been a leap of faith—absolute faith in the Mystery and heart knowing sourced from the power of Divine Love. I trust that power. And I trust in my own Sovereignty.

Special Gift

A NOURISHING MEDITATION

Do you long to connect more deeply with the power within and around you—a power that is rooted in love? Do you desire connection to that root to feel supported as you move through your daily life? Begin your day with this nourishing meditation to deepen into greater connection—to be nourished by the power, wisdom, and love that envelops you and all life.

This is how you begin to awaken your radiant heart.
This is how you reclaim your essence, joy, and power.

Access here:
www.elsaperezdean.com/sovereign-unto-herself

Elsa Perez Dean is a Certified Facilitator of The Practice®, a modern-day Priestess, Temple Guide, and Gatekeeper, based in the 13 Moon Mystery School, a Soul Nourishment & Sacred Wellness Designer, Founder of Nourish, Heal, Shine! and The Sanctuary of the Radiant Heart temple.

Elsa is passionate about inspiring women to reconnect to their inner wisdom, reawaken their divine radiant heart, and reclaim their joy.

Elsa believes in integrating all things beautiful and good for you. She began her journey as an interior designer in corporate architecture, bringing beauty and structure to corporate and healthcare spaces. Her work encompassed her passions, including sustainable and environmental design and creating spaces to enhance connection and wellbeing. After 20 years in design, Elsa followed the call to reimagine her life. She pursued a degree in nutrition and became a holistic dietitian nutritionist and wellness coach with the mission of guiding women back to their vitality. Under the mentorship of Michelle Long, Elsa became the first Certified Facilitator of The Practice® sharing her love of deep connection in women's circles. Elsa has always desired to share her gifts on a deep and spiritual level to make meaningful change in the lives of others.

Elsa's journey of healing and transformation led her to deepen into the wisdom teachings of the Divine Feminine as an Initiate in Devotion and Apprentice Focalizer within the 13 Moon Mystery School along with her mentors, Eden Amadora, Elayne Kalila Doughty, and Ariel Spilsbury. Today she weaves all of her lived and learned experiences in devotion to love.

Elsa channels her joy by creating the sacred spaces and offerings that provide soul nourishment and guide women back to their own divine heart and their fullest expression of beauty, love, and empowerment. Learn more about Elsa and her offerings at **www.elsaperezdean.com.**

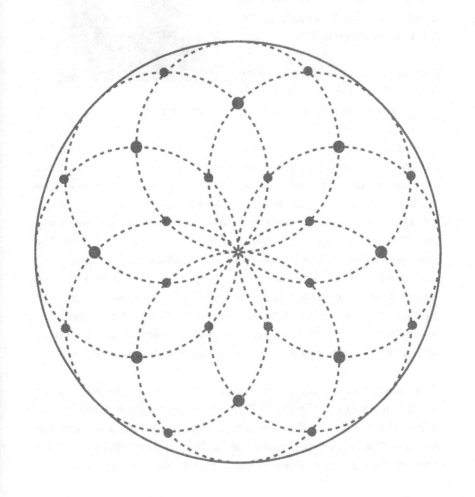

From Struggling Servant Girl To Sovereign Six-Figure Queen

BY TARA PRESTON

I was not the woman on this path who came into six figures within the first year of her business. You know you hear and see this so often in the online world: Women building businesses at quantum speed.

It's all fabulous indeed, and all the power to you if that's your story. It certainly wasn't mine. Far from it. Yet, I wouldn't trade my story for anything.

In fact, it was almost eight years ago that I stepped onto this path as a sacred feminine entrepreneur. In so many ways, as a younger thirty-something version of my current-something self, I still felt like a girl.

For so many of us, this path will bring up everything that is ready to be resolved and healed. Everything that can't come with us—as we rise into a higher vision of leadership and prosperity—asks to be worked through and released.

Nothing can prepare us for the challenges or even the numerous dark nights of the soul that this path may bring.

It's not always pretty, and sometimes quite painful as we strip, shed, and rebirth ourselves over and over again into the sovereign powerful woman that we know deep down we truly are.

I will say that the fulfillment, true freedom, and tear-stained cheeks of deep joy that are now common in my life have been so worth it.

Every layer of pain dissolved makes more room for the fully awakened passionate woman to emerge more self-expressed. In the case of my story, many moons ago, that woman was dying to be set free through a business and life she loved.

＊＊＊＊＊＊＊

During the first few years of getting my business off the ground and taking the big leap of following the call of my soul, it felt like all of my struggle patterns were illuminated instantly. I remember entering the online world terrified of being seen, yet feeling so called to share my gifts in the world. I wasn't able to allow myself to connect fully to my community in service through my gifts as I really hadn't owned the value of me yet, which made it difficult to really cultivate a connection to a community where I could contribute and have that circulate back to me through currency.

The disconnect was painful. I was pushing so hard, working so hard, and did not feel seen or compensated at all for my work in the world. This often created even more difficulty between my husband and I. I wanted my dreams so badly, and yet the struggle put pressure not just on me financially but on us.

My money story was rooted in lack, which meant there was never enough. And I mean NEVER enough. One time, after I had burned through all my savings, I found myself searching for coins around the house to go buy coffee. I was too embarrassed to tell my husband that my business was barely creating any income despite my best efforts for over a year.

I was also full of self-doubt when it came to trusting my soul to lead in business. Who was I to claim that power, saying exactly where I wanted to go, and exactly how I would get there? I questioned everything all the time, which created confusion and distrust in my own sacred leadership as the true queen of my business.

It was constant pushing, and constant pulling, looping around back to square one on my sacred path over and over again—for what felt like an eternity. Things eventually shifted when I learned to get control of my mind, rewriting my old stories into new ones with Akashic Record subconscious clearing work. As I started to understand the power I had over my experience, I began to give less power to the limitations that my mind kept presenting me with.

I had story after story that would loop me back around to square one on my path—stories that told me that I wasn't good enough to have what I wanted, that it wasn't safe to trust new ideas, that making money had to be difficult. I perpetuated these stories by believing in their power. The stories kept me safe in the comfort of the old self for a long time.

Finally, I was forever seeking the financial support of my husband (even though I wanted nothing more than to stand on my own two feet). I would lean on him over and over again, secretly wanting him to take care of me. I so often felt deeply abandoned by the masculine and, interestingly enough, by money. Later, I realized ho much the two were so intimately connected for me. I was so afraid of showing up powerfully in my business and life, and totally cut off from the true source of money while looking for it outside of myself.

> *The little girl inside of me so desperately sought to feel safe,*
> *loved, and provided for by an external masculine.*

While my husband loved me, I knew it wasn't his job to take care of me. However, the wounded feminine in me had other ideas...

Way back then, even in my thirties, I was *still* playing out little girl patterns.

Life was happening to me.

People-pleasing patterns ran rampant through my life.

I never felt worthy, seen, heard, or loved—from others or myself.

I felt abandoned in my quest to live the life of feminine prosperity I was being called to live.

But still, I kept showing up and doing the work that I needed to do to heal generations of ancestral trauma, patterns, and disempowerment, often rooted in patriarchal rule going back thousands of years.

The truth was, at the very core of my human experience, I was wounded, disconnected from my power as a sovereign woman, and limited by common illusions. I felt a deep sense of separation from something more powerful than the human experience with which I was being confronted.

While this new path of service was challenging, it was some of the most rewarding work I have ever done in my life. I had found the Akashic Records for a reason, and I knew that serving women who wanted to feel full, connected, and authentically self-expressed was work that I would find deeply satisfying.

The Akashic Records are my most sacred tool and spiritual ally for this path. This ancient source of love, wisdom, and deep healing works at soul level to clear karmic patterns right at the very subconscious, soul root. It is by far one of the most powerful methods for assisting our collective evolution in today's world.

In my former life, I had worked in retail as a professional make-up artist for high-end cosmetic lines. My salary, even at the best of times, rarely rose over $3,800 a month. Through my twenties that was acceptable, but later, as a mother with dreams of experiential travel for her daughter, *and* a woman with even bigger desires of her own, a flourishing business became my desire and focus.

I knew that if I really wanted to experience the freedom of creating my life on my terms, then money would have to be a part of the equation.

I knew that I would have to grow into the woman who was living that vision.

I knew that fully harnessing my own creative potential as a divine feminine woman would be a vital part of my unfolding—*if* I were to truly take the throne of my business empire.

No more limitations.
No more playing small.
No more putting the needs of others first.

No more relying on the masculine to save me.
No more hiding my power.
No more undervaluing my gifts, voice, and vision.
NO MORE.

The wounding ran deep, and I was tired of being pulled around by life.

······⌾⌾⌾······

As a little girl, I had parents who played out stories recreated from generations before. That trauma lived on through them, and I experienced a childhood of one with an absent alcoholic father who later would become homeless for many years and a mother who bounced around trying to find love in the arms of any man who could finally see her value as a woman.

Was it really any wonder, that as I am choosing a path outside the box of society, that ALL OF THIS would be asked to be healed? That as I rise into my crown power, all parts of my inner Queendom would need to undergo upgraded restructuring, in order to fully allow me to anchor into a paradigm where feminine prosperity would rule?

As I cleared past-life trauma patterns and present-life trauma patterns, my ancestral lineage and my childhood wounding shifted, making way for a new inner energetic template to support heaven on earth.

I reclaimed my divine heritage of wealth, remembering that nothing was outside of me.

The source for my own radiant rise was within.

I was not separate; I was a divine being whose beauty, power, prosperity, and sense of security was now unified from within.

My inner child was being held safe in the arms of the divine feminine and newly-resurrected divine masculine.

I experienced new levels of prosperity because I *was* prosperous.

I was more than enough, as a rich daughter of the Divine.

That was an integrated divine truth that became reflected in my reality. Anything else was just an illusion, and I no longer needed to buy into the lack that I perceived as so prevalent in today's society.

Rather, I could harness my creative power as a divine feminine woman and know with certainty that I had an unlimited capacity to create money, *on-demand,* based on my deepest desires.

As I allowed my divinity to fully lead, desire became the lead in my life and business. Desire began to fuel my life. The Goddess spoke through me in the language of longing. I would listen to the deep requests for greater divine expression through the physical experiences I wanted and knew with such certainty that God would always provide for any authentic desire that I had.

The doubt that clouded my path dissolved just as all the layers of limitation and pain had.

I rose, my inner little girl feeling safely held in the arms of the newly wedded internal feminine and masculine union.

I was reborn.

Free to create life on my terms.

Free to lead from a place of authentic desire and know without a doubt that the divine never withholds what is truly meant for me in this experience.

It's my job to claim it. To decide I am going to have it. And to show up visibly and powerfully as the Queen that I am.

As my sense of empowered new paradigm feminine leadership landed, so did 10K, 15K, and even 20K months.

Was this really me? The woman with inner child wounding who started off in retail? The one who struggled to make even $2,500 a month for the first few years in business?

Yes, *me.*

Yes, *you.*

Yes, *we.*

Our sovereignty is a return to unity.

You've probably heard one of the more popular universal laws that states: *As above. so below. As within, so without.*

This is a universal truth.

As we collectively heal past trauma, then break down the conditioning that separates us from our true divine feminine/masculine sovereignty and power, we one by one anchor into a new paradigm of prosperity.

As divine beings, we were never meant to be without.

We are meant to flourish. It is our natural birthright to experience prosperity with ease, and to create a life aligned with our values and desires. But this is not without effort.

At the core of my journey was a return to self and divinity.

My world as a young woman was fraught with the hardships of external dictation. I looked everywhere, just as my Mom had, for validation and a deep sense of value.

And just like my Mom, for a long while, I searched in vain.

I carried the pain of a world that I thought didn't see my beauty, so I looked outside of myself for approval, hoping someone would see me—and even pay me well! But this only resulted in more pushing and giving, and my ongoing relentless patterns of never feeling like enough, thus, creating an experience of never actually having enough.

Ah, the cycles...

Once I began to see myself, I healed. In the presence of my own divinity, I could sink into the *now* and anchor in new truths that would ultimately land me in a new experience of Self. The outside world became powerless as I reclaimed my feminine power.

When I could truly hold a mirror up to the beauty within, owning the value of not just my innate presence, but of my natural goddess gifts, *I remembered.*

I remembered that the world needs my gifts and that I deserved to be compensated well.

I remembered that I was a sacred feminine woman whose divine heritage is wealth.

I remembered that money is the energy of God and love, and that money, just like God, loves me and wants to be there for me.

And, finally, I remembered that God wants to be there for me, provide for me, and take care of me. That as a divine woman, it is safe for me to let go, trust the flow, and fully open to receive.

As I leaned into the energy of a higher divine masculine and opened my ability to receive, the currency of money began to flow with ease—through the web of connected channels—into my community.

I led in service through my sacred business.

Now, I have a spacious life that feeds me as abundantly as I feed (and serve) others in my community—through my gifts, message, and transformations.

Now, I have time for connection, self-care, family, and travel.

Life flows, flourishes, and circulates in a rhythmic web of prosperity that supports my sovereign feminine evolution.

Truly, isn't that the way it should be?

Tara Preston is the creatrix of the Flower of Life Akashic Healing System who over the past nine years has done approximately 5,000 Akashic reading and healing sessions. She is a six-figure spiritual business owner who has spent the last decade working with women at the soul level through one-of-a-kind life reinvention transformational packages and Akashic Record work. Tara now has a pros-perous, purpose-based business guiding women through major life transformations that pave the way for next-level prosperity, leadership, and legacy work all while rooting deeply into the power of their divine feminine magic. She incorporates the spiritual healing power of the Akashic Records and many other healing tools and feminine embodiment practices to assist her clients in healing deep collective feminine core wounds and soul-level rooted patterns. By doing this, she is able to facilitate deep and transformational work that allows her clients to feel free, powerful, and beautiful in the expression of their purpose in both life and business.

Women quickly feel empowered to step into the spotlight of their lives through Tara's work, then claiming what it is they truly want without apology, while attracting their deepest desires with greater ease and pleasure!

Over the past two decades, Tara has discovered how empowered women feel when they are given space to authentically self-express, whether that authentic self expression is through using their voice, claiming their dreams, sharing their gifts, or presenting themselves in a way that they feel really expresses their unique essence, truth, and power.

Before finding the Akashic Records, Tara worked as a professional natural beauty make-up artist. Tara helps her clients deeply connect to their intuition, inner beauty, and soul's vision by working with their natural feminine cycles. She believes that when women root into this intrinsic power, while valuing their divine gifts, and trusting themselves they naturally flow into greater evolution of their authentic expression.

Tara holds a space of love and non-judgment, allowing women to feel safe as they go deep into those messy and imperfect places inside themselves, re-calibrating their life and work so that it nourishes them to the core.

Learn more at **TaraPreston.com.**

Special Gift

21 Day Akashic Heart-Centered Journaling Practice

This practice includes a pre-recorded guided visualization and prayer audio that will connect you into the beautiful field of living intelligence, and drop you into your womb, heart, and higher self wisdom. Imagine drawing forth wisdom from *all* of your power centers as a Divine Feminine woman! With these tools, you'll open to this loving source of high frequency energy.

Access here:
www.akashicwomenschool.com/akashicjournal

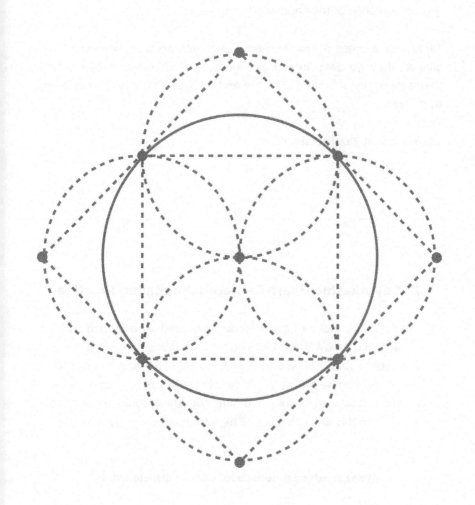

Being Sovereign Means Being "Never Not Broken"

BY LETTIE SULLIVAN

There is a goddess in the Hindu pantheon named Akhilanda. In Sanskrit, it's pronounced *Akhilandaeshvari.*

Ishvari translates as "female power" or "goddess" and akhilanda means "never not broken."

She is meant to be known through personal experience. Not a lot is written about her, but those who embrace this powerful archetypal energy have access to a consciousness that uses pain to purposefully transform while you are in your most vulnerable state.

The teaching is that you will not break—because you were never not broken in the first place. Like the tectonic plates that shift and move over the magma in the earth's crust, we, too, are subject to life's bursts of destructive energy that break us apart only to create anew.

Let me share with you how I consciously embraced this potent goddess energy in my life to maximum effect, resulting in true freedom, liberation, and sovereignty in my mind, body, and soul.

In 2010, my world was broken open. A close relative who was staying with me tried to take their own life. I didn't see it coming. I knew they were feeling a bit down, but would have never suspected they would take it that far. I came home from work to find absolute chaos. Their mental state was such that they blamed me for their predicament and even went so far as to say I actually *wanted* them to die.

There had always been talk in my family about my mother's generation being cursed. True, we had been through hell, seemingly through no fault of our own. Every kind of trauma imaginable was wrought upon not just my mother and her siblings but also on my generation, their children. Poverty, violence, drug abuse, sexual abuse, murder, infanticide, mental illness... you name it, my family experienced it. Nowadays, I know that our family wasn't all that unique, especially in the black community, where we were at the effect of some very severe government policies, the crack epidemic in the '90s, and systemic racism and economic oppression.

As the youngest of my mother's children, so much of what was happening was never explained to me. There seemed to be constant chaos and emotional upset, fear, and an unrelenting hunger in my belly. I received approval from the adults around me for being quiet and unobtrusive, almost invisible. I found comfort and safety in my invisibility and became masterful at blending into my environment. It took many years to outgrow this very counterproductive mindset and behavior pattern.

With my siblings being almost a decade older than me, the impact of our family drama was more acute and damaging for them. Counseling and therapy, something that "white people did," was frowned upon in the black community. The underlying truth was that many couldn't afford to pay for treatments that were deemed "non-essential," and therapy was one of those. One had to be seriously injured or profoundly affected to even seek medical care, unless they were fortunate enough to have a "good job with benefits." As African Americans in the workforce, those jobs were in short supply.

To bring some sort of peace to our dire state of affairs, my mother turned to religion. In her mind, God was a "Wonderful Counselor" and "Protector"—the one you turned to in times of trouble. She would pray, and all manner of miracles would transpire. Whether it was food assistance, money in the knick of time, someone opening their home to keep us from sleeping in a car, or a last-minute spot opening up in a homeless shelter. "God will provide" was something that I heard repeatedly from my mother as a response to my inquiries about what we would do and where we would go. My steadfast belief in God now is mostly because I saw the demonstration of Divine interventions in extreme times of need too many times to count during my childhood.

As an adult, my first order of business was to get as far away from the "chain of pain" as I could. It became important for me to break the cycle of poverty and dysfunction.

Don't get me wrong; there was plenty of love, connection, and family unity in my upbringing. My mother, a strong matriarch and the eldest of her siblings, took on the task of looking out for her nieces and nephews and her siblings as much as they would let her. Our home was always open to extended family and a few close friends when necessary.

Overall, though, my intention as an adult was to blaze a new trail that put some distance between me and the destructive past I witnessed as a child.

After graduating from high school, I moved eight hundred miles away from my family. A clean break. A fresh start. I figured I had nowhere to go but up.

About five years into my independence, family members started migrating to my part of the country. With their arrivals came the same dysfunctional communication patterns, emotional outbursts, and drama. I began to think that maybe there was something to the idea of being cursed after all. Little did I know that generational trauma was passed down through our DNA, a fact that science has only recently discovered.

When I started having children, I became more obsessed with breaking the cycle of emotional chaos and financial hardship.

Instead of turning to religion for emotional stability, I looked into alternative spiritual practices. This was at the height of Oprah's "Live Your Best Life" movement. The New Age was in full bloom, and I went *all* in.

We weren't raised to seek any sort of counseling unless it was from the pastor of our church. We definitely were *not* encouraged to meditate or do yoga or any kind of Eastern practice that fell outside of traditional Christianity.

When I began to engage in these practices, I was first chastised and then ostracized by some of my family members. There was fear for my soul and that of my children. The superstition was palpable and the condemnation real.

At first, it hurt. There was so much good coming from what I was doing. My quality of life was improving in all ways. The tone and tenor of my mental and physical health was at a high octave. It was as though I had a force field of well-being around me. I wanted to share it with everyone in my life.

In hindsight, I can see that I was a zealot. Naive and optimistic with joy goggles on. From the outside looking in, it seemed too good to be true. Except I really believed in all the New Age stuff I was learning. I had a loving marriage to an extremely attractive man, a strong and healthy body, good job, nice car, house, clothes, social circle, vacations, all the trappings of a "good life." My zealot-like nature was producing results in my life.

I opened my home to my extended family and then fell right back into the old program, the old family dynamics. The programming ran deep. The wounds still festered, despite all the spiritual practices.

In the aftermath of the suicide attempt, I called into psychic Sonia Choquette's show on Hay House Radio. It was the first time I had ever gotten through, and I saw it as a sign from the Universe that I was being supported. She gave me a live reading on the air.

The first thing that Sonia said was that my first three chakras were completely out of alignment. She told me that in her mind's eye it was as though I had a huge gaping hole in my solar plexus chakra and my root and sacral chakras were covered in mud. She acknowledged the trauma I had been through without me telling her anything about me. Then she sent me her book *True Balance* so I could begin to learn about my energy body and how to bring it forward into harmony. When the signed copy arrived, I couldn't wait to dive in.

The book was a comprehensive set of inquiries and practices to get into relationship with each of the seven major chakras. While I had an awareness of what these energy centers were, it was very basic knowledge. My intuition began to inform me during my first read through that I needed to take as much time as possible with each chakra, to be complete with each one before moving on. Being a speed-reader, I had never really engaged with a book that way.

What I didn't realize was that I would spend more than a year healing each of my chakras and, therefore, the area of my life governed by that energy. Permanently.

It took nine years to consciously heal and get into a right-relationship with each chakra, but the end result of the journey is complete liberation in my consciousness and an experience of being sovereign at all levels of my Being. There was no script to follow, just a scavenger hunt with the Universal Intelligence/God/Source/Spirit. All I knew for sure was that when I was done with the energy work of a particular chakra, there would be a clear sign to move on. Every experience necessary for the embodiment and understanding of the chakras were brought to me via synchronicity.

The coincidences began within a few weeks of me starting the book. My root chakra was first up. I knew that I needed to heal old wounds from my troubled childhood. My intuition guided me to start with a clean slate. Some friends of mine were raving about a cleanse and how they were bursting with energy after just a few days. So I purchased an 11-day full-body detox kit from a friend who was a wholesale rep for the company. I also was introduced to Debbie Ford's 21-day Consciousness Cleanse book. With my journal in hand, I chronicled my journey of fasting, blending shakes, doing forgiveness work, and crying buckets of unshed tears. While writing this story I went back and re-read those journal entries, marveling at what a difference a decade makes. Many of the declarations I made for my life have come to pass.

On the other side of my physical and spiritual detox I felt completely renewed! It was like I had a blank canvas on which to paint my life. My purge revealed that I was carrying around a burden of my family lineage that wasn't even mine. Programming and beliefs about what was possible for myself and my life that were untrue and self-defeating.

Being the Capricorn I am, I took full responsibility for the spiritual baggage that I had inherited and set out to climb to the mountain top of freedom and liberation. I knew that if I didn't heal and transmute the negativity, it would be passed on to my children and the cycle would continue.

While working with a client to declutter their home, I was given an old set of CDs from a Nightingale-Connant course in shamanism taught by Peruvian shaman and Dr. Alberto Villoldo, PhD. What I remember most about listening to the course was that it never felt like I was learning something new. It was more like I was remembering things I had always known. When we got to the disc about essential shamanic practices that included Soul Retrieval and Illumination rituals, I was certain that a soul retrieval ritual was exactly what I needed to start to heal my root chakra.

Where does one find a shaman in a city like Chicago? As luck would have it, I was taking a class at my Spiritual Center and had been partnered with a woman I did not know well. We were tasked to pray and check in at least once per week. When I told her my story of listening to the CDs and wanting to have a soul retrieval, she informed me that her husband had studied with Dr. Villoldo and referred their dear friend, one of his classmates, to me to perform the ritual. How's that for synchronicity?!

On November 6, 2010, I parted the veils between space/time and journeyed through the spirit realm with my new shaman-friend, his drumming partner, and my husband, who was there to ground me. We met in the community room at my spiritual center, appropriately called the Zen Den. It was after hours and we were trusted to lock things up after we were finished.

The drumming began and my shaman and I laid on the floor next to each other. Our hands and feet lightly touched as he led us into meditation. Even going through my journal, I couldn't tell you what he said or how he said it. I just remember clearly the drum beating like a heartbeat. Then I remember the visions I saw. It progressed in three phases.

First, I went back to the past where my three-year-old self was standing in a sea of broken glass screaming and crying. I was scared, unprotected, and lost in a swirl of chaos and discord. No one paid me any attention. The adults in the house were arguing and fist-fighting, a large glass coffee table had been broken and no one bothered to get me out of harm's way. This was the original place where a part of my soul splintered off. I don't remember how I got out of that situation because I was so young. But the vivid recall of the house and the furniture and the fear was palpable.

After my soul loss, the memory was locked away. It became our work in the Present to call that part of my soul home. I comforted my wounded inner child and let her know that she was safe now, supported, and free from harm. Before then I would have extreme reactions to being around people who were arguing and fighting. I know now this was a form of PTSD. The sensation in my body after the retrieval was like taking a deep exhale. I had dug up a toxic, petrified root from the past and it had left behind fertile soil for me to plant new seeds.

The second vision was from a previous incarnation. While this was not a clear seeing vision, it was a deeply vivid remembrance of a series of movements and actions I had taken repeatedly over a great deal of time. It was the sensation of preparing for participation in a ritual. The vision was of myself in a room with candlelight and privacy. I lifted a heavy, velvet-like cloth. It was folded much like an envelope or a cloth diaper. I pulled open the left, right and center panels to reveal an ornate gold necklace with a pendant in the center that was a large amethyst shaped like a crescent moon. I placed it around my neck, felt its coolness against my skin and its heavy weight. Then, like I had done countless times before, I donned my priestess robes. Clearly, this was a retrieval of my lineage as a ceremonial Priestess. At the time, I was not participating in any such work, yet it felt so natural, so familiar. I knew somehow that one day I would be reunited with this necklace. I have been searching for it ever since.

As we came out of the trance state we had been in and began the process of unpacking the journey we had been on together, my shaman shared what had been revealed to him as a direct transmission for me. He said that he was given an ornate box to give to me. Inside was a large, luminous pearl. The message was that the pearl symbolizes all the beauty accumulated by the hardships and challenges I had faced and that I was as unique and priceless as the pearl because of all that I had been through. All I had to do was receive, unconditionally, the beauty and radiant essence that remained.

My husband was there as my witness as I wept cleansing tears. He had kept me anchored to the present moment and as I traveled beyond the veil, and it was greatly comforting to know he was right there by my side. My soul retrieval left me feeling rooted into my present life. Free from the past and whole and complete in a way I had never felt. From that day forward, I was ready to proceed on my chakra discovery and reclamation journey. No matter how long it would take, I was committed to seeing it through to the end.

Over the course of nine years, I healed and embodied the energy centers in my body, finding places within that appeared to be broken and loving them into wholeness. Whenever I was ready to move to the next chakra, the process of synchronicity brought me experiences and people aligned with exactly what was necessary.

I spent more than a year spotlighting each chakra. Building, repairing, and amplifying my light body. Becoming the sovereign priestess I am today. Unlearning and peeling back layer after layer of old programming, trauma, dissolving the ego and bad karma. It has been the most impactful spiritual/ emotional/mental education of my life. Wholly guided by intuition, faith, courage, and unshakable trust in the God of my understanding.

It seems only fitting that the final initiation for my crown chakra began on 9/9/19 with a pilgrimage to Egypt called Return of the Goddess. Nine is the number of completion. The itinerary was to journey up the Nile from Aswan in the south to Cairo in the north and stopping at temples along the way, which happened to correspond energetically to the 7 chakras of the human body. At each stop we would sing the temples awake and anoint each other with sacred oils and work with the Goddess for deeply transformative work.

We were a group of twelve women and five men. Some of us were deeply mystical and fully ordained, practicing Priestesses. Others were significant others on their own spiritual paths. We even had a teen with us, bringing a wide-eyed, fresh perspective to our extraordinary journey.

Chanting and toning inside the sacred temples was at the heart of our practice. We also carried sacred essential oils and participated in rituals of anointing, prayer, and meditation. There were advanced instructions on how to shield and work with the unseen realms. Egypt has a very active non-physical dimension that must be respected.

It was clear from the start that this pilgrimage was divinely orchestrated for the completion of the journey I had begun in 2010. I had been preparing myself for nine years to return to the land where I served in previous lifetimes to retrieve my soul parts. Not just as a priestess but also an architect, artisan, and cultivator if some sort. The memories of past lives would flash into my present moment awareness like being in my peripheral vision. I would have lucid dreams every night when I slept. Never in my life had I felt so alive and integrated. It was the most expansive, profound, and transformative experience in my life.

Our journey culminated in the King's Chamber in the Great Pyramid of Giza. We entered after it had been closed to the public. Our private time was reserved for two hours. Though it would not be appropriate for me to describe here what was done in the King's Chamber, there is a recording you can download of our group chanting with the full effects of the pyramid's echo creating magic with the tone of our voices. We were attuned to a particular frequency of 432hz and centered in our vow to walk as Love. To amplify Love on the planet. The King's Chamber initiation and the entire pilgrimage fine-tuned my chakras from root to crown and truly created an ascension level event.

As I write this, I am only six months removed from the experience. I went to Egypt like a set of Russian dolls, split in two halves and nested but the sizes were out of order with tops and bottoms mismatched. I returned from Egypt with all of my dolls neatly nested within, representing my past, present, and future selves finding their way back to order and harmony. My chakras spin in alignment radiating well-being and Love. I now approach each day with joy and gratitude, knowing that I am centered in the kind of sovereign power that only comes from a deep heart-knowing and resonance with the truth of my very Being:

I am One with ALL That Is and I am Never NOT Broken.

*During the entire pilgrimage in Egypt the words to this poem began weaving themselves into my soul. I completed it on our last full day in Cairo.

Egyptian Night

A golden sky and pink horizon is the last caress
of the sun
Absent the rays and heat, the rocks, trees and
beings have begun
to welcome Darkness in lazy haze, on a breeze
bringing relief from the scorching day
Now there is no sun, no moon, the space in
between
A pregnant pause before the underworld's cave.

Pisces moon rising over the Nile, silvery light
reflecting on the water
Activating my soul, both light and dark matter
Bringing forth the remembrance of that which
is beyond
Secrets discovered yet undisclosed
Revelations held in repose
Fragments fusing, Goddess musings
Open and also refusing.

Tidal pull, ethereal light, ancient mind will
amplify
Mirroring day in the Egyptian night, feeding
shadows with moonlight
Embracing the wonder of your relation
To the sun, the earth, the womb-holding ones
elation
Oh Egypt! Your beauty, your secrets, your pain,
Your riches, your gifts, your presence reigns
In the rulership of my heart and soul returning
to me all that was lost...

Temporarily...

Lettie Sullivan specializes in life transitions. As a Professional Organizer and life coach with 13 years experience in private practice, she is a veteran at supporting families and businesses to create organized systems and to clear clutter.

Lettie is whole unto herself. A sovereign queen, stepping into her power to support the establishment of a new social consciousness. A writer, speaker, leader, mystic, and Practitioner, Lettie is the Creatrix of The Goddess Ministry whose mission is to anchor spiritual practices centered in the Divine Feminine archetypes, metaphysical principles and cosmic time cycles.

Lettie is a bestselling author and inspirational speaker. Areas of specialty include families with children on the Autism spectrum, seniors downsizing into assisted living, and entrepreneurs who work from home.

Learn more at **LettieSullivan.com**.

Special Gift

LUNAR ENERGY DYNAMICS: WAXING & WANING

Activate lunar cycles, create rhythm in your life, and catalyze your manifestions with this video.

Access here:
https://bit.ly/LettieGift

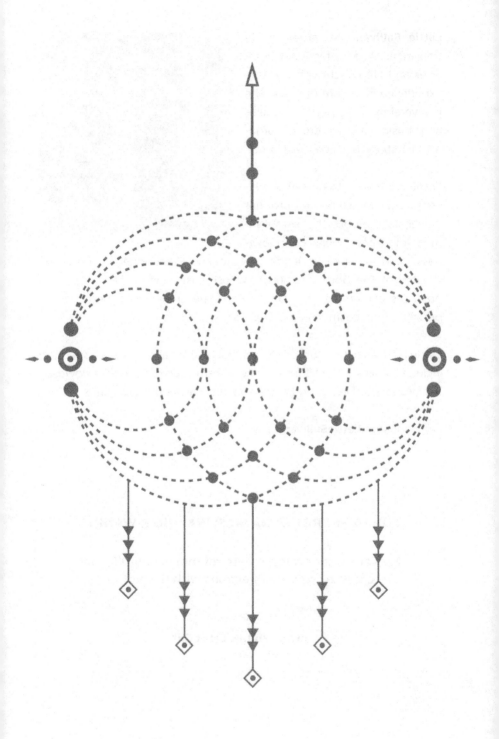

Easy Joy: Remembering the "More" of Who We Are

BY ADRIANNE SPIRALLIGHT

"Elephants."
What? I keep walking.
"Elephants."

I stop and turn around. I'm standing alone on an inexplicably empty patch of hot, dirty, cracked and crowded Thirteenth Street sidewalk. There is no one close enough to have spoken to me. I shake my head and resume my stride. Abruptly, I am jarred to a halt again, this time by a booming *tick-tick-tick* echoing loudly in my head, as if the white rabbit himself were flattening his pocket watch against my ear. "Elephants. Elephants never forget."

I am six years old, standing in the summer sun on a newly blacktopped driveway, trying to scrape tar off my faded and patchy carnation pink ball. I look up to the sky suddenly and say, "Oh!" Then I smile.

"Sorry," a woman mutters as she bumps past me. Thirteenth Street swims back into my perception in all its steamy, crushing, horn-honking blare. I stand there, swaying and blinking in the bright light, swerving pedestrians swearing at me.

Elephants, I whisper to myself. *Elephants never forget.* But I did.

·······⚭·······

At first, it was just memories of a memory. It was me, at twenty-six, surfing hazy waves of recall, remembering me, at six, remembering that moment, holding it close like a treasure, excited to share the wealth, and thinking, *I understand now. I understand it all now and I'll never forget.* Sometimes, I can still feel the shock of that memory, how it catalyzed an instantaneous recalibration of self, startling me into awareness of an intriguing other, perhaps truer, me, existing invisibly right alongside the one I recognized and performed every day.

Like the afternoon, a month or so into my freshman year of college, when I bounced into the ID checkpoint at my dorm and spent thirty minutes chatting with the security guard and the other students who came through, before I headed to my room. Halfway up the stairs, the walls of my mind were suddenly splashed with enormous, red, neon graffiti letters: I'm not shy! I just spent half an hour idly talking to strangers—I'm not organically, unalterably shy!

In that gray, institutional-concrete stairwell, my psyche was granted reprieve from the life sentence of solitary confinement my misguided family had unjustly pronounced upon me—and I, having no other guidance, had accepted. It was a joyous release.

So I was familiar with the phenomenon of discovering that I'd always been someone other than who I had been told I was. But this was different. This was mysterious. This held vast implications, extending, perhaps, beyond my own private life. Yet, as much as my astounded adult-self wanted to re-collect every part of what I knew at six, I also felt an unsettling hesitation. Like an in-rushing wave with an unseen undertow moves powerfully forward and undeniably back at the same time, part of me disbelieved and feared that memory. It only took a couple more moments of recall to figure out why.

I am so excited about my epiphany, I gush it all to the first person I see, my neighbor from across the street, who is several years older than me. When I'm done, I plop back on my heels in the grass, smiling, ready for her to grab my hands with delight or jump up and pirouette down the lawn. Instead, her long, mute stare cuts me, and I become afraid. "You're crazy," she slices the silence with absolute finality. And then she gets up and stalks away.

"Don't you see?" I say, "Time, death and eternity, I know how they work!" I›m standing between my chair and the dinner table, my hands stretched out, pleadingly, but my words are lost in the cacophony. Am I invisible? Suddenly, my father pauses his monologue; he noticed me! My mother›s voice rushes into the vacuum left by my father›s deviant calm. «Adi, don›t talk crazy,» she says, her tone at once dismissive and brittle. My father turns in his chair to face me, his eyes two dark drills, spinning faster and faster. «A-dri-anne,» his lips and tongue carefully measure the full length of my name, his gaze holding me like a hypnotist, «You can›t know that. Nobody can.»

But. What. If. I. Do.

As young children, we have long discussions with invisible friends and build rockets to Mars and space stations out of plastic bricks and tubes; we watch fairies dancing in the violets, communicate silently with animals and trees, and are willing to draw a sphinx, even if we've never seen one. Adults call this "play" or "wild imaginings" and label it frivolous and immature, certainly in comparison to the important worries preoccupying their minds.

But, what if, at six, I actually received information I "couldn't" know? What if it was something significant, something adults didn't even imagine could be perceived? What if that is true of all children? What if each of us, walking around in adult-suits, has access to far more than we have been taught to reach for, remember, or value?

Most people's lives are peppered with the inexplicable, yet we are trained to just shrug it off: synchronicities and déjà vu, "weird" ideas that tickle the backs of our brains, impulses we can't justify, intuitions we can neither prove nor measure, passions we can't trace, insatiable curiosities that drive us, deep loves that seem to come out of nowhere.

What if that nowhere is actually some place? What if some vital part of us lives in that place? What if our early child-selves display uncanny creativity and wisdom because they are still in deep communion with those invisible, ephemeral parts of who we are?

And what if, as adults, we could have contact with that "more" of ourselves— live in an easy, natural dialogue with "unseen us," as we did when we were children? How would that change our lives, our cultures, our worlds?

I've been asking these questions since that day on Thirteenth Street when I spontaneously remembered that I used to know the answers. I haven't managed to recall all the intricacies of my suppressed childhood epiphany, but the quest that memory set me upon has been utterly life-altering. In fact, because the journey was catalyzed by such a quirky, enigmatic piece of my childhood, walking this path is not only authentically *me*, it's deeply and lastingly empowering.

······⌘⌘······

Even though I do not now possess as full a grasp of the Infinite as I did at six, the winding road of remembrance has brought me potent perceptions. I see that, in the beginning, there is The One, or Source, desiring to be aware of itself. But, when you are everything, everywhere, simultaneously, how do you self-reflect? How do you... evolve? So The One diversified, creating the only thing it could: more of itself, fractals of its own consciousness.

Humans are but one kind of fractal consciousness in the infinity of All That Is. We are a special type of consciousness, though—we possess the ability to forget who and what we truly are. We experience the fear that arises out of separation from Source, yet we are coded for the ecstasy of remembering our true nature; we desire the sensation of connection—we've even named it *love*. The tension produced by these opposing emotions propels us to seek, using our physical senses to explore life in form, our minds to generate preferences and ideas, and our hearts to lead us into alignment with others, and with the more of who we are. This is a deep creation dynamic, and it expands the very fabric of existence.

⸱⸱⸱⸱⸱ ♾ ⸱⸱⸱⸱⸱

Our talent for forgetting and remembering is linked to the fact that each of us is one being who possesses (at least) two points of conscious awareness.

Imagine a beam of light spreading out as it gets further away from its origin. We'll call that starting point *Source,* the light represents the vibrational energy of Source and, as it travels, it creates and illuminates existence. Now picture that light passing through lenses, like those on a camera. Since the beam is broad, it can flow through multiple lenses at once; since the light is bright, an individuated ray can pass through a string of lenses in succession and still be potent and visible, though it may dim a bit from one lens to the next. Our consciousness is the product of Source energy passing through two lenses in a line: The Ethereal Self lens, which we recognize on a spectrum as instincts, gut feelings, intuition, muse, soul, embodied god/goddess; and the Material Self lens, which we know as personality, mind, or ego.

The lenses have the effect of filtering how Source energy perceives. The Ethereal Self is like a camera lens with a short focal length and high f-stop. It's closer to Source and can handle a lot of light while maintaining focus equally on many things at once, even if they are at varying distances. It has a wide view, so it can "see the bigger picture." The Material Self acts like a camera lens with a longer focal length and a low f-stop. It's really good in dim light situations and concentrates its sharpness into a small area, highlighting the details, texture, and contours of a subject while blurring everything else in the picture. The angle of view is narrow, further focusing attention on the subject at hand by cropping out anything extraneous.

Reliance on only one of these lenses may well yield an interesting or beautiful picture, but it will never represent our whole view. We need the Material Self's narrow focus, with great magnification of detail, in order to manage and fall in love with the nitty gritty of our physical existences, and we need the wide angle and long depth of field of the Ethereal Self to see and fall in love with the variety of life around us and to receive the full flow of energy from Source.

This is how we are constructed—our lenses of consciousness built to work in effortless synergy. When these lenses are in alignment, we feel fantastic. We experience our abundance and know our worth, we thrill to the bliss of vitality and unconditional appreciation, we are inspired and excited to explore and create, and we radiate love.

Misalignment of our lenses leaves us feeling cut off, scared, alone, and disempowered. We try to compensate for that loss of connection to Source by looking to relationships, jobs, and other activities to prove our worthiness. But it never quite works, at least, not for long. We can't fabricate an internal sense of value with outside things, but we can plug into the more of what we already are and live lit up from the inside!

This is the sparkly magic of early childhood. Young children haven't lost connection with their Ethereal Selves, because human society hasn't had the chance to talk them out of it. Kids don't have full capacity to navigate the physical world on their own, but they do have full ability to receive Source energy, to dream, and to believe their dreams are important and worthy of becoming manifest. They experience themselves as fully creative, and they radiate the ecstasy of being at once both cosmic and physical.

That natural joy, which we call *child-like*, is our birthright. We are Source consciousness that chose to come into the physical to experience Playground Earth, but we never meant to lose contact with where we came from.

As adults, we feel the pure happiness of a baby's smile and it lasers through our to-do lists and our mind chatter and ignites our remembrance of easy joy—but it's temporary. We are survivors of many years of training, convincing us we can't know something we weren't taught by another human, dogs and trees don't talk, and fairies are a myth.

It's as if human society gives us a cruel choice: deny the part of yourself that isn't material and you can belong or maintain your connection with the ethereal and sacrifice your place in the manifest world.

You can't be here and be whole. Nobody can.

But. What. If. We. Are.

The last time I spoke with my friend Jillian, she told me that when she was a kid she hoarded all her allowance and chore money to buy postcards and stamps. She would hand write a card to every tourism bureau she saw advertised, asking for packets of visitor information, which she hungrily consumed. A few days after our chat, she headed off in a Dodge Ram pick-up, pulling a camper filled with art and computer supplies, to journey across the USA on her own for an entire year. This is her retirement gift to herself.

My friend Simone was raised by parents who were educators and social-change makers. Her early enchantment with cars didn't seem to fit well with the family ethic, so she abandoned engines and got a degree in psychology. After an unsatisfying stint as a counselor, she decided to go back to college; this time, though, she'd follow her rogue passion and study to be a mechanic. Since she already had a B.A., she was unable to receive financial aid for an associate degree, so she never went to automotive school. That was thirty years ago, but when I told her I was musing about quirky childhood fascinations, this story sprang immediately to mind, and I could hear regret ring in her voice.

Childhood passions deserve to be recalled, cherished, pursued. They are vital breadcrumbs on our paths to remembering our wholeness. They are place markers, energy vortices, signposts, treasure chests, genie lamps.

In my own life, I can see my youthful, deep bonding with pets leading to my work as an animal communicator, the many hours I spent ceremonially stirring buds and leaves and dirt into big pots of water heralding my practices of herbalism and sacred Goddess mysteries, and the "time, death and eternity" moment presaging my ability to read energy fields and channel guidance for people from their Ethereal Realms.

But I walked very indirect routes along the way, mired in forgetting and censure and fear. I frequently felt conflicted and riddled with self-doubt. Sometimes trauma wiped all human options away, gifting me the invitation to believe again in my Ethereal Self; sometimes its low, insistent voice persuaded me into new directions. Luckily, my early love of writing, dance, and all things art 'n crafty granted me socially acceptable avenues of access to the Ethereal, after my direct contact was repudiated and I blocked it out. I've come to appreciate that all art forms, especially non-commercial, amateur, "unskilled" endeavors, possess the capacity to bring us into connection with Source. That's why making art so often feels like love.

•••••◦∽Ɛ◦•••••

We all long for wholeness and authenticity. We deserve to experience abundance, ecstasy, and easy joy. We want to express the fullness of ourselves and have that touch the lives of others in positive ways. We need open, active connection with our higher octaves to do that.

The good news is, our Ethereal Self is permanently focused on the wide-angle view and always bathing us in the unconditional love that is Source. No matter who or what in the human world turns away from us, we can never actually be rejected; we are held in, we are made of, that beam of love, and we just have to relearn how to attune with it.

The truth of who and what we are is here, walking right alongside us down the street, holding hands with our inner child, waiting for us to remember.

So, what does any of this have to do with elephants?

An elephant herd's survival is attributed to what science deems the uncanny recall ability of its leader, the oldest female. Her confident responses to danger and stress indicate vast internal resources. Not only does she track the movements of every member of her own group, up to seventy individuals, she can recognize outsiders, both friends and foes, no matter how briefly or how long ago she met them. Apparently indelible inner maps of all terrain she has ever traversed enable her to guide her charges to far distant areas of water and food in times of local drought and famine.

But the influence of the matriarch elephant's mysterious powers does not end with her own herd. Elephants are a "keystone" species: their presence creates and maintains entire ecosystems, making life possible for a huge variety of fauna and flora. Without elephants, those ecosystems would fail.

It's time, beautifully human Fractal of The One,
to claim your elephant memories.

More Flower of Life Press Books

The New Feminine Evolutionary:
Embody Presence—Become the Change

Voices of the Avalonian Priestesses:
Hearing the Call of Essence

The Wealthflow Code:
Finding Focus, Freedom and Balance
in a High Stress Career

Pioneering the Path to Prosperity:
Discover the Power of True Wealth
and Abundance

Sacred Body Wisdom:
Igniting the Flame of Our Divine
Humanity

Plant-Based Vegan and Gluten-Free
Cooking with Essential Oils: Your
Kitchen Companion for a High-Vibe Life

SocialEyes Together:
Ignite the Power of Belonging

Emerge:
7 Steps to Transformation
(No matter what life throws at you!)

Sisterhood of the Mindful Goddess: How
to Remove Obstacles, Activate Your Gifts,
and Become Your Own Superhero

Path of the Priestess:
Discover Your Divine Purpose

Sacred Reunion:
Love Poems to the Masculine and
Feminine—an Anthology

Rise Above: Free Your Mind One
Brushstroke at a Time

Menopause Mavens:
Master the Mystery of Menopause

The Power of Essential Oils:
Create Positive Transformation in
Your Well-Being, Business, and Life

Sacred Call of the Ancient Priestess:
Birthing a New Feminine Archetype

Self-Made Wellionaire:
Get Off Your Ass(et), Reclaim Your
Health, and Feel Like a Million Bucks

Oms From the Mat:
Breathe, Move, and Awaken to the
Power of Yoga

Oms From the Heart:
Open Your Heart to the Power of Yoga

No Country for Truth Tellers:
Follow the Story the Wild Horses Tell Us
about Ourselves, Globalization, and the
Ability of a Storyteller to Persevere

The Four Tenets of Love:
Open, Activate, and Inspire Your
Life's Path

The Fire-Driven Life:
Ignite the Fire of Self-Worth, Health, and
Happiness with a Plant-Based Diet

Becoming Enough:
A Heroine's Journey to the Already
Perfect Self

The Caregiving Journey:
Information. Guidance. Inspiration.

The Pathfinder:
A 365-Day Interactive Journey

Navigating in the Dark:
Personal Stories and Techniques for
Overcoming Challenges and Saying
Yes to Life

Made in the USA
Monee, IL
10 December 2020